Cultivating the New Nature:

Growing into the Full Stature of Christ

Kevin M. Rice

Cultivating the New Nature: The path to the Full Stature of Christ
Copyright © 2021 by Kevin M. Rice. All Rights Reserved.

All rights reserved. No part of this book may be reproduced in any form or by any electronic or mechanical means, including information storage and retrieval systems, without permission in writing from the Author. The only exception is by a reviewer, who may quote short excerpts in a review.

Cover designed by Uriah Ocean Peterson
Author's Photo by Racheal Mahon

Kevin M. Rice
Visit my website at www.EternalKingdomInternational.com

Printed in the United States of America
Crown City, OH

First Printing: May 2021
Eternal Kingdom International Publishing, LLC
LIBRARY OF CONGRESS
LCCN: 2019915642
ISBN- 978-1-7341088-0-4 - Paperback
ISBN- 978-1-7341088-1-1 - eBook
ISBN- 978-1-7341088-2-8 – Audio

Copyright © 2021 by Author.
All rights reserved.
Printed in the United States of America at

Dedication:

This book is dedicated to my wife - Sandra - and kids - Seth, Salina, Kenzie, and Khloe - for their tireless support and love over the years. I also want to thank all the people who sowed the Word of God into my life and called out the greatness God has placed within me. A special thanks to my pastor, Chuck Lawrence, for believing in me, even in the midst of insurmountable resistance. His friendship and vision have inspired me and helped me to grow in grace and truth. I am also thankful for my church family at Christ Temple Church in Huntington, WV (CTCWV.com), for their wonderful friendship and support. And finally, I would like to express my gratitude to my mother and father for raising me in the church where I could experience a life-changing encounter with Jesus Christ.

"Therefore, if any man be in Christ, he is a new creature: old things are passed away; behold, all things are become new."

(2 Corinthians 5:17 [KJV]).

Contents

Prelude 1
Chapter One 5
    Genesis of New Life 11
Chapter Two 13
    The Old is Gone 15
    The Task Ahead 17
    Our Spiritual Eyes Are Now Opened 18
Chapter Three 22
    World Changers 23
    We Can't Learn to Walk Without Stumbling 24
    Do Not Delay—Grow Today 24
    How Do We Accomplish Our Higher Calling? 25
    His Good Pleasure 27
    Begin in Jerusalem 28
    We are Valuable 30
Chapter Four 32
    The Meanwhile 34
    Great Cloud of Witnesses 38
    Don't Just Settle 40
    Dwell on the Future, Not the Past 42
Chapter Five 45
    Epigenetic Influences 48
    Nutrition 51
    Infections and Infestations 53
    Trauma 57
    Environment 59
    Cultural Factors 61
    Emotional Factors 65
    Chronic Diseases 67
    Ordinal Position in the Family 68
    Growth Potentials 70
    Toxins 71
    Producing the Optimal Environment 73

- Chapter Six 76
  - Hope 78
  - Will 82
  - Purpose 84
  - Competency 86
  - Fidelity 88
  - Love 91
  - Care 93
  - Wisdom 95
- Chapter Seven 97
  - The Apostle's Process 100
  - The Prophet's Process 101
  - The Evangelist's Process 106
  - The Pastor's Process 108
  - The Teacher's Process 112
  - The Combined Process 115
- Chapter Eight 121
  - Servants of Righteousness 124
  - Born of Righteousness 127
  - Flee Unrighteousness 129
  - A Baby No More 132
  - Correction Brings Righteousness 134
  - Live for Righteousness 136
  - United in Righteousness 138
  - A Righteous Mind 141
- Chapter Nine 145
  - The Qualities of Maturing 152
  - Not Being Led by Feelings 154
  - Distinguishing Other Voices 155
  - Not Being Dependent on Others' Approval 157
  - The Benefits of Maturing 159
  - The Eminence of a Mature Son of God 162
  - Full Circle 164
- References 167

Prelude

"But they heard only that he who persecuted us in times past now preacheth the faith he once destroyed"

(Galatians 1:23 [KJV]).

We have been given a new nature through Christ. We have undergone a metamorphosis that's transformed us from darkness to light. The old life we used to live consumed the God-given potential bestowed on us by the Creator. Our time, talent, and resources were wasted in pursuit of things that took us farther from our destiny. Much like a butterfly in a pupa stage consumes the plant that would one day provide life-sustaining nectar, what once our lives destroyed now, we are ordained to cultivate and protect. We once channeled all our energy and time to fulfill our own desires at the cost of others. Now we have been called to be a servant of Christ to those we once used and abused. Once we're born anew, we're ordained to cultivate and protect the new life, the gifts, and callings bestowed on us by God.

This statement holds great meaning to a person who has experienced the transformation that comes with a new birth experience. I've experienced change many times in my life. Change doesn't always feel good, but changes are necessary.

I remember beginning kindergarten. I didn't want to go. Most of my life had been spent at my mother's and my father's side. I was introduced to a new location where my father and mother were absent. There were new people and new experiences—everything was different.

Going away to school required an abrupt and unwelcome change in my life. I was thrust into a new environment filled with new people and new expectations. It was colorful and loud, and overwhelming. Everything was different from what I'd known before, but I had watched T.V. and thought I knew what school was supposed to be like.

I vividly remember not knowing where to go after lunch. We were playing on the playground between two identical buildings. One class was in one building and the second class was in the other. When recess was over, I went to the wrong building.

I had seen kids change classes in T.V. shows, so I thought it was time for me to change classes, too. I sat there nervously, looking at all the new faces. I was wondering why all the other kids did not change class when they were supposed to. I thought maybe they made a mistake, so I waited, trying to take in all my surroundings. Finally, my teacher came in the back door looking for me.

I made a change when it wasn't needed, frightening the teacher and myself.

There is a process to change. Things happen in stages. The same is true with our Christian walk. We begin our life as babies before maturing. All the while, we are moving toward the full stature of Christ. Unfortunately, many get lost along the way, or they try to take steps out of order.

We all begin our life as sinners, alienated from God. We have the capacity to do things that can destroy the person God wanted us to be. I can look back over my life and see all the mistakes I've made and all the things I've done that didn't work to build my future. I destroyed relationships and destroyed opportunities, but God had a plan for me. I just couldn't see it.

When God finally transformed me, the things of my past couldn't support the new creation I had become. I needed to learn to live another way.

Many people today struggle with how to live a Christian life. Many religions have made a list of rules to follow, but God never meant for us to live according to regulations to earn His grace. He desires us to grow and mature into his image and likeness.

Within this book, I hope to provide believers with the understanding that they have been given great potential through the conversion of their soul. This potential empowers us; it imparts a knowledge of who we're meant to be in Christ; it instructs us in wisdom regarding the steps we should take to progress toward maturity; and it equips us with the tools required to successfully grow into the full stature of Christ.

This book is written for you who have already undergone a soul conversion and are looking to maximize your God-given potential and improve yourself and your faith. If this is you, enjoy the journey ahead.

Chapter One

ReGENEration – Spiritual Genetic Transformation

"Not by works of righteousness which we have done, but according to His mercy He saved us, by washing of regeneration and the renewing of the Holy Ghost."

(Titus 3:5 [KJV]).

As we embark on this journey, we must begin with the knowledge that we're of tremendous value. We're not simply marred vessels God noticed lying in the gutters of the earth, waiting to be picked up. We're not simply filthy vessels that have been washed clean of our past, only to be displayed on a shelf as a work of art. Neither are we purposeless vessels to be counted as trophies at the end of time by who collected us—God or Satan.

We're vessels that have been washed and restored back to our original purpose—earthen vessels with God-given callings, resources, and limitless potential. We each have unique skill sets and a vital part to play in the Kingdom of God.

I grew up on a farm in southern Ohio. My grandfather purchased the old farm after my father returned from the Vietnam War. When I was four, my father began to build a house on the part of the farm where I live today.

I can clearly recall my journey to school one morning when I was a little boy. It rained the night before, and the ground was wet and muddy. My brother and I had to walk about a quarter of a mile to the bus stop in front of my uncle's house. We would meet my cousins there and wait for the bus to arrive.

On this particular morning, my brother and I were running late. We walked quickly through the edge of the woods to get to the bus stop. On the way there, I slipped and fell into the mud. It was dark, and I couldn't see how muddy I had gotten. I didn't have time to run home and change, and even if I did have the time, I had few school clothes to change into.

I continued to the bus stop and climbed onto the bus.

When I got to school, I didn't want anyone to see how big of a mess my clothes were. I kept trying to hide the stains from everyone, but it was hard to cover the dried mud on my pants. I felt embarrassed. I didn't want anyone to know I came to school with dirty clothes.

On the bus ride home, I tried to sit by myself and not talk to anyone. When I got home, I rushed to take off the clothes and put them in the hamper before my mom noticed.

Looking back, I can't recall anyone saying anything to me about the dried mud on my clothes. No one stared at me. No one called me names. No one seemed to notice. All the shame, guilt, and condemnation were within me. I was still the same person with the same friends. The teachers thought I was a joy to have in class. My parents loved me.

The perception I had of myself affected my interaction with the world around me. The shame came from knowing I was better than my current state.

My mom always made sure we had clean clothes to go to school. I was not meeting my mom's expectations, and because of that, I was not meeting my own.

We've all had thoughts suggesting we're meant to be more than we presently are. We have an intuition inside of us that spurs us toward the knowledge of a greater purpose. Often the thought doesn't translate to tangible actions.

The philosopher Immanuel Kant once wrote, "Thoughts without content are empty, intuitions without concepts are blind ... Only through their union can cognition arise." (Kant 1787, B75-76)

We must be empowered by the knowledge that we're of great value. We must possess a clear understanding of the characteristics of our new nature—a new nature we have received through the redemptive work of God in our lives. Only through embracing these elements of who we've become can we ever begin to nurture our new nature and move into our unique purpose.

Before we can become what God intended us to be, we must first arrive at the revelation that we have potential within us. Aristotle once stated, "The actual which is identical in species though not in number with a potentially existing thing is prior to it" (Cohen, 20001049b18-19). Here, Aristotle explains the potential involved in becoming what we originated from (image of God) lies within us. Potential is the key. We can become like Christ because we're born again into His likeness.

Through the experience of being born again, we have been changed. This transformation has taken the attributes of our fallen nature and replaced them with the potential to express the nature of Christ. One could say we've undergone a spiritual genetic transformation. The spiritual DNA of our fallen nature has been replaced or repaired with the original nature God gave to man in the garden.

Our spiritual genetic transformation doesn't occur by the works of man. This transformation is a gift from God. Our faith in God leads us to call upon Him and receive Him intimately into our hearts. This faith is counted as righteousness. The missing, mutated, contaminated, and repressed part of our spiritual nature, lost to carnality, is genetically repaired and replaced by the Spirit of God when He imputes His righteousness into us. Now regenerated, we have the potential to manifest the characteristics of God.

Now that is a mouthful of words. To put it simply, a caterpillar doesn't resemble what it'll be when it's an adult. The butterfly will express far different genes than those of the caterpillar. However, recessive genes lie dormant within the caterpillar, waiting to be activated. These genes are what make a caterpillar change into a butterfly.

When Adam was created, he had the potential to be the image of God. However, Adam and Eve made a terrible choice that changed them forever. The potential to be like God was damaged by sin. They were mutated and unable to fix what they'd corrupted.

That is what Christ came to earth to rectify. He created a way in which man could be cleansed of the mutagenic power of sin while awakening the dormant traits God had placed within man during creation.

Only through the leading of the Spirit of God can we begin this process. The process begins with repentance and progresses. Through the process of the new birth, we are spiritually transformed.

> *"But to him that worketh not, but believeth on him that justifieth the ungodly, his faith is counted for righteousness. Even as David also describeth the blessedness of man, unto whom God imputeth righteousness without works."*
>
> (Romans 4:5 [KJV]).

In this scripture, the Greek word for "imputeth" is *logizomai*. The root of this word is *logos*. *Logos* is translated as "word" in the New Testament. It means logic and reason—literally the logical conclusion of one's actions or reasoning. *Logizomai* implies the reckoning of logic or passing logical intent to one's account.

At this point in the spiritual conception, God passes the logic and equity of His character to our spiritual account. Through His *logos* (word), He places in us an internal consistency (or conscience) that is equitable with the traits of God—His righteousness. Our spiritual DNA is transformed, and we now have the potential to display the traits and attributes of God's character. We become a new creature with a renewal of purpose, destiny, and design. A resurrection of the original, garden nature given to us in Eden is accomplished by God's *logos*, becoming flesh and redeeming men.

His *logos* must become the essence of our existence. As our lives begin to express His *logos*, we'll see the expression of His nature.

In all honesty, it's taken me many years to understand this concept. I grew up in an organization that prided itself on the holiness standards set forth by its leaders. Growing up, I learned to play my part. I followed every rule and did what I was told. At an early age, I knew God. I would talk to Him as a friend. I would play in the woods and have conversations with Him.

When I was twelve, I remember feeling God in my heart telling me to be baptized. I was a good boy and hadn't done many things wrong, but I felt the need to repent and be baptized.

Over the next few years, I went through some rebellious phases. I began to see the hypocrisy of some of the people in the church. I could play the role, but I didn't fit in with the church people.

The youth group had their cliques, and they weren't very friendly. To make friends, I learned a new role. I began to learn the culture of the public school. I wore two masks: one at church and one at school.

One day, I was the first student on the bus to go home. Allen, one of the boys from my grade, entered the bus and started a conversation with me.

"You don't cuss," he started.

"What do you mean? I do, too."

"I haven't heard you cuss," he said.

I then proceeded to unleash terrible words from my mouth.

He looked at me in shock and took a seat as other students started to get on the bus.

I sat by the window of the bus, thinking about the conversation and all the emotions it stirred up in me. I had never used those words before. They felt wrong in my mouth, but in the moment, I thought I needed to use them to prove that I fit in.

A few days later, I overheard Allen speaking to another boy in our grade. The words came out of his mouth as they had mine. I began to realize I'd never heard Allen use a cuss word.

I recall this story because, after that experience, I never used those words again. I came to realize the relationship I had with God was on display for those around me. I hadn't mentioned God or talked about church, but they knew there was something about me that was different.

After that event, I began to seek a deeper relationship with God. Even though the road from a child of thirteen to a man has been marked with many missteps and failures, I've realized God isn't trying to judge and condemn me. He's trying to nurture and correct me so I can mature into His likeness.

Genesis of New Life

> *"Not by works of righteousness which we have done, but according to His mercy He saved us, by washing of regeneration, and renewing of the Holy Ghost."*
>
> (Titus 3:5 [KJV]).

In Greek, the word for "regeneration" as used in this passage is *paliggenesia*, which was created using two Greek roots: *palin*, meaning "again," and *genesis*, meaning "birth, beginning." This implies the beginning of a new genus, new genes, new DNA. The Greek word means "the coming of a new birth" or "born again, regeneration." Through the new birth, God has "re-Genesis-ed" mankind, restoring the spiritual man back to the original garden nature He intended at creation. What an amazing concept it is to know God's mercy restores us through being born again—a transformative process bringing our spiritual nature back into good standing with God's original design!

Once new birth occurs, the maturation process begins. This transpires through the renewing power of the Holy Ghost. In Greek, the word used for "renewal" is *anakainosis*, which is created from two Greek roots: *ana*, meaning "completing a process," and *kaino*, meaning "making fresh or new." The use of this word emphasizes the completion of the process as the Holy Spirit makes us new.

Through conception and birth, the process of life begins.

My wife and I have experienced the birth of five kids. One of our children died at birth, but the miracle still amazes me. Even more amazing is the transformation that occurs when someone is born again.

God can take a drug addict and make him a world evangelist. God can take a murderous, religious zealot and make him a church planter. Through a spiritual new birth, change will occur.

> *"But we all, with open face beholding as in a glass the glory of the Lord, are changed into the same image from glory to glory, even as by the Spirit of the Lord."*
>
> (2 Corinthians 3:18 [KJV])

This internal genetic code lays the foundation for the metamorphosis I'll discuss later. As we place this new nature in an environment saturated with the presence of God, we'll begin to be transformed into His image and purpose by the Spirit of God. It's not instantaneous; it's a gradual process. We change and progress from one degree of glory to another.

Chapter Two

Metamorphosis

"Therefore if anyone is in Christ, he is a new creature; the old things passed away; behold, new things have come."

(2 Corinthians 5:17 [KJV]).

Just because we've been birthed into the family of God with His traits of righteousness encoded in our spiritual nature doesn't mean everything we do from that moment on is righteous. We must take ownership of our new nature and grow into the fullness of Christ. As with our physical nature, the manifestation of our spiritual genetic traits takes time. For instance, a person who is a gifted singer has the genetic traits required to sing from birth, but those traits must be developed and honed to optimize the vocalist's gift.

Without God, we can't resurrect our garden nature. It takes a supernatural experience. Through Christ, God created a way for our garden nature to live again. Our spiritual nature, through the catalyst of rebirth, comes alive unto God. When we give up our carnal nature through faith, repentance, and baptism, God transfers His nature and the mind of Christ to our account. This new, spiritual nature will transform the corruption in our hearts and manifest Godly righteousness. Paul references this transformation when he writes:

> *"And be not conformed to this world: but be ye transformed by the renewing of your mind, that ye may prove what is that good, and acceptable, and perfect, will of God."*
>
> (Romans 12:2 [KJV]).

Paul originally uses the Greek word *metamorphoo* for "transformed" in the verse above. This word is derived from two Greek words: *meta*, meaning "change after being with," and *morpho*, meaning "changing form in keeping with inner reality." Properly translated, this word means "transformed after being with or transfigured." The spirit comes alive and is made anew. Man's inner reality is changed to experience the *metamorphoo* and is transformed to reflect the newly received nature.

Paul speaks of this transformation experience again when he indicates this change transforms us into God's glorious image.

> *"But we all, with open face beholding as in a glass the glory of the Lord, are changed into the same image from glory to glory, even as by the Spirit of the Lord."*
>
> (2 Corinthians 3:18 [KJV]).

Once again, Paul uses the word *metamorphoo* when he states, "we are changed." The process of metamorphosis is spiritual transformation, which causes our outward expression—our thoughts and actions—to align with our new internal nature. This metamorphosis is an external manifestation of an internal, spiritual transformation. For our thoughts and actions to mirror those of Christ, we must experience a spiritual genetic reprogramming through regeneration by God's mercy.

The Old is Gone

> *"Whereby are given unto us exceeding great and precious promises: that by these ye might be partakers of the divine nature, having escaped the corruption that is in the world through lust."*
>
> (2 Peter 1:4 [KJV]).

Through the potential placed within us by our spiritual DNA, we now have exceedingly great and precious promises. The scope of these promises is not only of the eternal life to come but the amazing destiny God has designed for our lives while on earth. This great potential establishes the foundation for our development. If we allow the process of metamorphosis to progress and develop according to God's design, we'll be partakers of His divine nature. Our once dominant lust and corruption, which promised a destiny of death and destruction, will no longer have a grip on our lives. As Paul states, we are new creatures through God.

> *"Therefore if any man be in Christ, he is a new creature: old things are passed away; behold all things are become new."*
>
> (2 Corinthians 5:17 [KJV]).

The fleshly desires that once ruled us are not in control of our lives or choices anymore. We're in the process of spiritual transformation; we begin to experience metamorphoo and reflect the traits of the Creator. This transformation requires a process of maturity as we grow toward the full stature of Christ. It is our aspiration; we have a lot of maturing to do.

We've been given the power to develop this spiritual potential. Christ has eradicated the hostility between the law and our carnal nature. We have a new life void of condemnation and enmity of the law. Our original garden nature has come alive as we have undergone an internal repair. The spiritual genetic mutations imposed on us by our carnal nature have been corrected and brought into the perfect design of the Father. We now have a spiritual genetic code that, if expressed, will transform us into the likeness of Christ.

> *"And have put on the new man, which is renewed in knowledge after the image of him that created him:"*
>
> (Colossians 3:10 [TLB]).

Once alienated from God, mankind was unable to come into His presence for renewal. Through the blood of Christ, this barrier was destroyed, and we now have unrestricted access to the presence of God. Our relationship is renewed, and we can approach our Father for guidance, wisdom, and comfort. He readily wraps His loving arms around His prodigal child, as if to say, "Everything is going to be okay. I am here with you until the end."

> *"Having therefore, brethren, boldness to enter into the holiest by the blood of Jesus,"*
>
> (Hebrews 10:19 [KJV]).

What a great privilege we have as children of God! Not only were our sins forgiven, but the sentence of spiritual death and eternal separation from God has been removed. Eternity in Hell was exchanged for Heaven. We are now children of God with direct access to His presence in this earthly life.

> *"And that ye put on the new man, which after God is created in righteousness and true holiness."*
>
> (Ephesians 4:24 [KJV]).

As described in this passage in Ephesians, only when our hearts are set apart solely unto God's design and purpose are we truly holy. This internal holiness will naturally inspire external actions, which manifest God's righteousness. To possess an exterior display of holiness without the internal state of good standing with God is hypocrisy. We're created to be holy as He is holy. Through regeneration, we've been made righteous; we've been given the potential to obtain a state of holiness and separation unto God's purpose.

Adam and Eve originally lived within the confines of the garden, maturing and preparing to step into their role. We must do the same now with this new nature. We need to be nurtured by our Father and position ourselves in an environment that inspires success, where we can grow from infancy into the full fruition of His plan. This seed potential was not given to us by man; it came from God so we could become the image of His glory.

> *"But as many as received Him, to them gave He power to become the sons of God, even to them that believe on His name; which were born, not of blood, nor of the will of the flesh, nor of the will of man, but of God."*
>
> (John 1:12-13 [KJV]).

The Task Ahead

How do we become all that God has intended us to be? Even though a child may be born with the greatest potential, he will never rise to all he could be without intentional mentoring and nurturing. We must become deliberate in regard to our destiny. God must be established as a priority in our lives; He must be first and foremost in all we ask, do, and think. Our spiritual genetics are programmed for a successful outcome, but we must have our spiritual eyes opened to see the Lord as He truly is. We must be transformed by His glory and mentored by His Spirit.

Today, many people do not see a spiritual side of the life they live. They only perceive what the natural eye can see in the physical realm. The same is true with spiritual sight. Some only see evil because it's all they've ever experienced in their lives. Others may believe in the existence of a god but do not see clearly which deity is the one true God. Our predispositions keep us from seeing with clarity. By regeneration, we have the ability to train ourselves to discern good from evil.

> *"But strong meat belongeth to them that are of full age, even those who by reason of use have their senses exercised to discern both good and evil."*
>
> (Hebrews 5:14 [KJV]).

Our Spiritual Eyes Are Now Opened

> *"Wherefore henceforth know we no man after the flesh: yea, though we have known Christ after the flesh, yet now henceforth know we him no more."*
>
> (2 Corinthians 5:16 [KJV])

To truly have our spiritual eyes opened, we must change our perspective. We must stop evaluating what we see through the lenses of past experiences and patterns of thinking. We must allow the Word of God to become the lens through which we see the world around us. The more we know His Word, the easier this becomes.

The new nature God has given us through new birth into the Kingdom didn't remove our ability to choose wrong over right. We still maintain the ability to live according to our lustful, carnal nature. In the Book of Ephesians, Paul insists we be "renewed in the Spirit of our minds" and that we "put on the new man." This is the only way we'll cultivate our destiny and purpose in Christ. We have the privilege and responsibility to choose good over evil. The scripture is replete with instances that denote our requirement to make a choice. Therefore, we must choose to be renewed. We must choose to be led by the Spirit. We must choose to nurture our new nature.

> *"This I say therefore, and testify in the Lord, that ye henceforth walk not as other Gentiles walk, in the vanity of their mind,"*
>
> (Ephesians 4:17 [KJV]).

> *"That ye put off concerning the former conversation the old man, which is corrupt according to the deceitful lusts; And be renewed in the spirit of your mind;."*
>
> (Ephesians 4:22-23 [KJV]).

This new man can only grow if we allow our minds to be separated unto God's purpose. We must meditate upon what is truth and act in a manner that demonstrates the wisdom of God. We've been born into a new spiritual man, but our mind still possesses the same thought patterns and memories present before God's redemptive work. If unchecked, these memories of past behaviors and fleshly thinking can become dominant again. Our thoughts must be subjected to our spirit, and our actions must align with

God's wisdom. We must "put on the new man" daily. As this new nature dominates, we'll be endued with power from on high.

Our spiritual man is reborn unto God's purpose, and we have the righteousness of God grafted into our spiritual being. With this righteous power comes great potential. Scripture states that God "who quickeneth the dead and calleth those things which be not as though they were." We are able to speak into existence things in our life that do not align with God's destiny or are none existent (Romans 4;17 [KJV]).] The things of the spiritual realm are more real than those things of this temporal world. However, we also have the ability, through our thoughts and actions, to recall the traits of our buried carnal nature. We must cast off those former behaviors and separate ourselves from our sinful past.

"Wherefore come out from among them, and be ye separate, saith the Lord, and touch not the unclean thing; and I will receive you."

(2 Corinthians 6:17 [KJV]).

Our mind and flesh are ever-present within us and aren't regenerated in the same way as our spirit. They must be transformed through metamorphosis. The memories of our past aren't erased, and the habits that once controlled us can still dominate us if left uncorrected. We must, therefore, crucify the passions and sinful nature of our old selves. It's a cyclical process; when we choose to speak life back into our old selves, we must crucify him or her once more.

"And they that are Christ's have crucified the flesh with the affections and lusts."

(Galatians 5:24 [KJV]).

We not only possess a new nature, but we also have great potential. Upon this foundational knowledge, we must build our spiritual walk. We must move from simply knowing we have a New Nature to acting with an awareness of our potential.

Chapter Three

The High Calling

"I press toward the mark for the prize of the high calling of God in Christ Jesus."

(Philippians 3:14 [KJV]).

The regeneration event of a child of God and the developmental processes following that regeneration impart the potential for greatness. The traits of our Creator are programmed within our spiritual DNA instantly as we accept the mercy and grace He offers through His sacrifice on the cross. Each newborn child of God has such great potential that a single chapter couldn't begin to explain what a newborn is capable of becoming.

The newborn nature is limitless in its potential when it's placed in a proper environment to grow. This inborn potential creates a drive within the newborn believer to manifest greatness. Within us is the very nature of a creative God, the one who calls things that aren't what we thought they were. This God of *logos*, who can envision the end from the beginning and whose logic exceeds the intellect of the wisest men, transfers His traits to His children. This becomes our calling: to obtain what is unimaginable to the world but is the very nature of the one who created it.

The creative nature of God works within our spirit, compelling us to this higher calling. Within each believer, there is a drive to do more, to reach higher. In the fallen state, the world tries to suppress the remnants of the desire that lies dormant in all mankind, the residue of our pre-fallen, garden nature. After conversion, the regeneration of the Holy Spirit awakens and intensifies this drive. It places within us not only a clearer vision of what we can become but also the realization and impartation of the indwelling of God's characteristics necessary for manifesting the vision of our God-ordained calling.

World Changers

God calls His children to be world changers. Each believer has the potential to live a life of honor and integrity and has the power to live a life that changes the world around them. Every unborn child of God, even the most wretched sinner in the gutter, has the spiritual calling to be a world changer. They are just awaiting the regeneration of their souls through the conversion of their hearts. Once this conversion occurs, the manifestation of God's children, once dormant, emerges, and the great potential within comes alive. The traits of God are implanted in our spirit, and the expression of our spiritual genetic qualities begins.

This overpowering motivation to fulfill a higher calling is within the hearts of every person redeemed by Christ. It drives us to do something above and beyond the world's status quo. This spirit refuses to let us be ordinary or mundane; we are appalled at the thought of being average. There is a power working within us, pushing us toward the exceedingly abundant plan God has for our lives. This is the mark of God's higher calling in Christ Jesus. We can attempt to ignore or suppress it, but we can never escape this calling upon our lives.

We Can't Learn to Walk Without Stumbling

Along our course of development, we may stumble and fall. We may face obstacles or opposition to the great vision longing to manifest within us. There are times when we may feel we are alone in seeing the potential within ourselves or within those we are trying to mentor. No matter the challenge, the truth remains that we are children of God. An opportunity to grow might be disguised as an obstacle.

As a baby begins to develop, there are a number of difficulties that must be overcome. The child must learn to crawl, walk, talk, and go to the bathroom independently. Each task poses its own set of unique obstacles. How can a baby learn to crawl if they haven't yet developed the ability to roll over?

Many times, we face situations we perceive as detrimental to our spiritual nature and the higher calling to which we are drawn. These hindrances are not always placed before us as deterrents. They may be developmental milestones charged with stimulating our spiritual growth, so we can cultivate a specific trait or skill required to reach our optimal spiritual health and maturity.

Do Not Delay—Grow Today

Often, children of God arrive at these points in their development and allow the obstacles to cause delays or stunt their spiritual maturation. During these times, some turn to alternate areas of their lives to fulfill the higher calling that burns within them. They may seek worldly positions, amass material possessions, or seek higher education in an attempt to fill the void left by the dormant, undeveloped potential. However, we can't assuage the higher calling of our regenerated nature with cheap worldly substitutes.

Only Jesus can satisfy the soul. We can never be satisfied until we pursue the calling we were designed to accomplish. God's children are created with an expected end, envisioned beforehand by the Creator. To reach the finish line and complete His plan, we must step up to the starting gate and begin to run. We can't reach our destiny without first beginning the journey! This great adventure awaits each of us.

Our trophy, our heavenly reward, is with the Lord in eternity. We're not of this world, but we've been called to this world for a brief time. Heaven is our home, but the earth is our current assignment. To complete our assignment, we must develop the skills and traits associated with the Kingdom, becoming mature children of God in this world. As sons and daughters of the Most High, we've been called to be Kingdom ambassadors and heavenly representatives.

How Do We Accomplish Our Higher Calling?

One question many people have is, "What is my calling?" All born-again believers have a calling, but some callings are more apparent than others. We have a set of unique Kingdom traits, specific gifts, or skills that we possess, and others do not. As these skills and talents begin to develop, our personality becomes more defined. In the context of the Kingdom of God, the same principle applies. There are some people who have an amazing talent with children, others who can orchestrate parking cars on Sunday, and some who may be skilled musicians who can lead a congregation into the presence of the Almighty. Each of us has an essential role to fill in the Kingdom of God.

The first step in manifesting the greatness within us is to recognize we all have a God-given calling. We may not know exactly what the final results of our calling may be. We may not even know the first step we need to take to catapult our calling to fruition. Until we recognize God has placed a great calling within us, we can never embark on the great adventure God has for our lives.

To actively pursue the calling God has for us, there are several things we must do. First, we must love God. Our relationship with Him must grow. The intimate time we spend with God is critical to the development of a spiritual ear, which is able to hear His voice and understand His leading. Just as God walked in the cool of the evening with Adam and Eve, He desires to walk and talk with each one of us. He desires to reveal His heart and His wisdom. He has said, if any man lacks wisdom, let him ask of God. The heavenly Father desires to take us under His arm and train us like a father teaches his son.

The second thing we must do is love people. There is no Godly calling on a believer's life that circumnavigates the necessity of loving our neighbors as we love ourselves. No matter how high we may go in life, no matter the worldly accolades we may achieve, if we do not love others, we are of no value to the eternal Kingdom of God. Our ultimate goal is to nurture our new nature until we grow into the full stature of Christ. If Jesus is the express image of God's love, and we are striving to mature into Christ's image, how can we fulfill the calling of God in our lives without love?

Our daily walk should exemplify the nature of Christ. Our daily speech should bear witness to the world that we are children of God. Our thoughts should focus on the characteristics of Christ. We should place before us things that point toward our heavenly destiny, not toward the ways of the world. God has promised us long lives and numerous blessings if we seek Him. We must seek the Lord in all we do.

We must also treat our bodies as the temple of the Holy Spirit. We should eat well and live healthily. We must care for the body God has given us to fulfill His plan. From the time we receive Christ as our Savior, our life is no longer ours to live as we choose. It's God's life, and He desires to live out His great plan through each of us. We must be faithful in caring for God's gifts entrusted to us. Although Paul stated that bodily exercise profits little, we must ensure we're in shape for when our calling is fully manifested. It will be much easier to fulfill our calling with a healthy, fit body.

His Good Pleasure

It's God's good pleasure to provide for all of our needs according to His riches in glory. We must realize everything that has been placed in our lives doesn't belong to us. We are simply caretakers of God's possessions. The cars we drive are God's cars, loaned to us to fulfill His plan for our lives. Likewise, our homes, our clothes, our finances are all God's. We are just the stewards of His Kingdom's riches. We sin when we hoard possessions and money, taking pride in what we claim is ours. These possessions are in no way ours; they are gifts from God that enable us to fulfill our purpose.

Once these financial and material items are placed by God into our care, they must be well cared for. He has blessed us with what we need in order to fulfill His design for our lives. Many people wonder why they are not prospering and may be facing financial difficulty. We must examine our motivations to fully comprehend the blessings of the Lord. If we're not seeking His Kingdom and His righteousness, then all of the things we believe we should have will be out of our reach. Our hearts' desires and the pursuit of our calling will manifest His blessing. God places within our lives the things we require to fulfill His purpose. If we aren't pursuing His calling, then we don't need anything that would aid in its manifestation. He promised to supply our needs. If we have food, shelter, and clothing, He has fulfilled his obligation. If we are in want of more things, we must seek Him, keeping in mind none of the things we possess are ours. They are on loan from God, and He could ask us to give them away at any moment. Our response to this should be according to His request. The earth is His and the fullness thereof; we are only stewards of the riches of His Kingdom.

Begin in Jerusalem

The people God has placed in our circle of influence are vitally important to our destiny. Our actions toward others are critical to the manifestation of the greatness within us. Our character and integrity are directly linked to our destiny, and we must strive to be of the utmost moral character. The Bible indicates the Kingdom of God is an ever-growing government, and we're ambassadors of that government. As such, our influence should grow daily as a manifestation of God's Kingdom.

God has also placed us in positions and roles to help develop the greatness He has planned for our lives. If we're janitors, we must be the best janitors we can be. If we're business owners, we must be the best business owners we can be. We must always perform the job set before us with excellence as unto God.

If we're parents, we must be the best parents we can be. The role of a parent is the greatest level of responsibility of any role in God's Kingdom. Inside every child of God is an inner voice speaking to us and encouraging us to be the best mom or dad possible. This isn't our own will or plan; it's

God's desire for us. He has placed within us the care of the future of His Kingdom. The kings, rulers, statesmen, priests, leaders, and world-changers of tomorrow are placed within our arms the moment we become parents.

Christian parents must be exemplary parents, a parent the world looks up to as models of great parenting. We've looked to the world long enough to define our roles and to show us how to raise our children. The world has given us many alternatives to occupy our children, so we can focus our time and effort on building our own lives. We have neglected the greatest call on our lives—that of being a parent. The world says it is permissible to park our children in front of the television for hours on end while we work on our next project for our career. Maybe we're not focused on our career, but we allow ourselves to be intoxicated by the latest scandal, reality T.V., sports, world news, or the like. God did not call on the television or electronic devices to parent our child. He called on us.

We're not just called to go through the motions of life. We're not meant to only be a wife, husband, daughter, son, employee, or church member. We are called to be the best version of ourselves the world has ever seen. This is the drive and motivation God has placed within each of us; it is who we are. We are being called to step up and live a life of abundance. If we commit ourselves to become the best at the position God has placed us in, we will grow.

The greatest step we can take toward fulfilling our calling is to become the best at what God has placed in front of us. Whatever our hands have been given to do, we must do it with all our might as unto God. We need to be the criterion and the benchmark for the position God has placed us in. As we cultivate and protect that which has been entrusted to us, God will expand our territory of influence and the scope of our calling. Many equate calling with the will of God, and it is God's will for us to step into our calling.

We are Valuable

We must understand that we have value. God didn't save us because He had no choice. We were not the last player on the field, and God reluctantly said, "I'll take him." No. He had a purpose and a plan for each of us from the moment we were conceived in our mother's womb. We aren't an accident. We aren't a stranger. We aren't an orphan. "Orphans of God" by Buddy and Julie Miller eloquently portrays this message in song.

There are so many times we forget we didn't call ourselves to repentance. We were moved by the Holy Spirit of God and drawn into His presence. We were presented with an opportunity to establish a relationship with the one true and living God. He has a plan for our lives. He has a higher calling for each of us. He doesn't make mistakes. We're valuable to His purpose.

> *"But even the very hairs of your head are all numbered. Fear not therefore: ye are of more value than many sparrows."*
>
> (Luke 12:7 [KJV]).

God doesn't define our value by what we have or the current state of our life. We must remember God doesn't call the equipped; He equips the called. There's a seed of greatness that God is calling out in each one of us. He sees us for our great potential, not our current flaws and failures. He has so much confidence in what we can become. He forgave us and placed within us the power to live out the calling He has planned for us. If God says you are great—and He does—His word will not become void. You are what he says you are.

Chapter Four

The Inner Sphere for Greatness: Cultivate the Seed

"And God said, Let the earth bring forth grass, the herb yielding seed, and the fruit tree yielding fruit after his kind, whose seed is in itself, upon the earth: and it was so."

(Genesis 1:11 [KJV]).

As we serve Christ, it's likely we'll have unrealized potential in our lives. We're filled with supernatural power. We don't have to work to attain it; it's already inherently inside each believer. However, this power is only a potentiality until it's placed in the proper environment.

In 2005 the director of the Arava Institute for Environmental Studies at Kibbutz Ketura in Israel, Dr. Elaine Solowey, an expert in desert agriculture, germinated an ancient seed. This seed was recovered decades earlier from a historic mountainside fortress called Masada. During an archaeological excavation, a researcher found seeds from a date palm tree that was over 2000 years old. The researcher cataloged the seeds and placed them into a drawer at a university in Tel Aviv. The seed spent years in Tel Aviv until Dr. Solowey rediscovered them and came up with the novel plan to cultivate the over 2,000-year-old seeds. From one of these seeds grew a male date palm tree named Methuselah. Nearly a decade and a half have passed, and Methuselah is thriving, along with a number of other date trees sprouted from other date palm seeds found at the same archaeological site and surrounding area. These seeds have reestablished an exinitic species of date palm and are currently reproduced dates (Sallon, Cherif, et al. 2020).

This date seed was filled with potential for 2,000 years, waiting to produce its intended fruit. Once placed in the proper environment and correctly cultivated, the seed could develop into its intended purpose. Similarly, we can carry the seeds of greatness even into death, never seeing the fruit God intended for our lives. Righteousness can lay dormant like potential seeds within us, never reaching its full stature without the proper environment and cultivation.

We see God's process for implementing intended outcomes is initiated with a seed. All things are given in seed form and must be cultivated. Our innate potential from the garden and our renewed potential attained through the regeneration of our spiritual nature both exist in seed form. This inner sphere of greatness—the "seed"—is the fundamental genetic code of our new nature. It must be provided proper nutrients, protected from harmful influences, and planted in the right environment to reach its maximum potential.

The ability to creatively manifest the glory and image of God to this lost and dying world is more than the pinnacle of holiness we move toward; it's also the fulfillment of the potential within us. This fulfillment requires directed, disciplined effort on our part to cultivate what we've been given. Working together with God's Spirit, we each can fulfill our role with the ultimate outcome: glory unto God.

Much like the shell containing the germinating natural seed, we must die ourselves for the seed to spring forth. Our old nature is pushed aside, and our new nature emerges and flourishes. This process is not instantaneous, nor is it effortless. It requires work and time for the new nature to thrive. However, the joy that is set before us far outweighs the labor required to manifest the greatness residing within each regenerated child of God.

The Meanwhile

The time from planting to harvest has periods when there's no apparent growth. However, on the microscopic level, millions of changes are taking place. To everything, there is a season, and for every season, there are specific environmental factors that must remain constant for optimal outcomes to transpire.

There may be times when it seems like life has come to a standstill. There may be times when it seems no physical growth occurs. Many of us remember our teen years when we waited anxiously for a growth spurt, so we could be as tall as others in our class.

Maybe you remember these seasons of slow growth in other ways: learning to whistle, enjoying bigger rides at the county fair, or learning a musical instrument. You may have wanted the training wheels off the bicycle, only to learn you couldn't keep your balance in the driveway. You tried and tried but couldn't make any headway on the skill you desired to master. Maybe you were counting days until you could get your driver's license, graduate high school, or marry the love of your life. Everyone has some point in their future they're anxiously anticipating that seems so far away. At times like these, it feels like no progress is being made, and time is moving at an arduous pace.

The time between one achievement and the next is the "meanwhile." There are many times in your development as a child of God when you will face a "meanwhile" season. Often, these times come with a test or trial—a lesson we must learn to transition into the next stage of development. The Bible even talks about these times of testing.

> *My brethren, count it all joy when ye fall into divers temptations; Knowing this, that the trying of your faith worketh patience. But let patience have her perfect work, that ye may be perfect and entire, wanting nothing.*
>
> (James 1:2-4 [KJV])

Tests aren't enjoyable. No one likes the process of failing. However, if we're never tested, we don't have the opportunity to assess where we're deficient in our growth. Assessment is a tool to point out where knowledge, understanding, and wisdom are lacking. The trials aren't meant to destroy us but rather to prepare us for the next step in our spiritual journey. If we don't pass a test along the way, we can rest assured we'll be tested again. Amazingly, we're assessed by "open book" tests and can ask the instructor of the class for help! The scripture tells us to ask God for assistance.

> *If any of you lack wisdom, let him ask of God, that giveth to all men liberally, and upbraideth not; and it shall be given him. But let him ask in faith, nothing wavering. For he that wavereth is like a wave of the sea driven with the wind and tossed.*
>
> (James 1:5-6 [KJV])

The "meanwhile" moments in our lives are cyclical for education, training, maturity, and assessment. Throughout the Bible, God has woven "meanwhile" moments into the lives of many people. For instance, God came to Abraham and Sarah in their golden years to share His plan and purpose for their lives.

When they were well advanced in age and childless, God told Abraham he would have a son by his wife, Sarah. Abraham was seventy-five years old when God gave him the promise of a son. Twenty-five years later, his son Isaac was born. For twenty-five years, Abraham was pregnant with a promise and didn't see it come to pass. Abraham and Sarah even tried to help God by taking matters into their own hands.

God used this time between the promise and the delivery to test Abraham's faith, to build a covenant relationship with Abraham, and to give him prosperity and the power to obtain wealth.

By the time Isaac was born, Abraham's faith had reached the level of maturity he had lacked twenty-five years earlier. When tested with the sacrifice of his son, he didn't hesitate. With unwavering faith, he knew God was able to provide Himself a lamb. At this moment, Abraham had matured spiritually into the father of many nations, even though he could not see them with his physical eyes. His spiritual maturity gave him the knowledge, understanding, and wisdom to speak life into his son, grandson, and great-grandchildren.

In another example, Joseph was seventeen years of age when he dreamed about the sheaves and stars. He was sold into slavery that same year when his father, Israel, was about 107 years old. Miraculously, by the age of thirty, Joseph stepped out of slavery and into the role of second-in-command of Egypt.

Seven years later, the famine began, and shortly thereafter, he revealed himself to his brothers. Joseph sent for his father, who presented himself to the Pharaoh at the age of 130. From the time of his dreams until their fulfillment, twenty-two to twenty-three years had passed in Joseph's life. During those years, Joseph became a leader with the character and integrity required to rule Egypt and provide refuge for his family.

Moses was born and protected from death as an infant. Eighty years passed from the days he spent growing up in Pharaoh's house to when he returned to Egypt to stand before the Pharaoh with Aaron, his brother. When he was 120 years old, he overlooked the Promised Land from the east side of the Jordan River. There were many "meanwhile" times in Moses's life, but during them all, he grew and developed the skills he would need to fulfill his purpose.

David was between the ages of ten to fifteen when Samuel anointed him as king of Israel. At age thirty, he was crowned king of the northern tribes of Israel, and a few years later, he became ruler over all of Israel and Judah. Multiple trials and tests appeared in David's life. There were many periods where it seemed he wouldn't see the manifestation of his rightful place as the king of Israel. In the midst of wars with other nations and fighting within his own kingdom, David held on to the promise. The "meanwhile" periods of David's life tested and trained him to become a great ruler.

Christ was thirteen years old when He first taught the scribes in the temple. His earthly ministry didn't begin until He was thirty. From the time He stepped into the temple to teach until the time He performed His first miracle at the wedding in Cana, He was in a "meanwhile" season. There were things in life He had to experience. He needed to receive earthly and heavenly training in order to fully step into His destiny.

Once we have glimpsed the destiny God has intended for us, we can rest assured all the events that will transpire in our lives are meant to train, develop, mature, condition, and equip us to fulfill our calling. As long as we're moving toward His purpose in our life and clinging to that promise by faith, it will come to pass in God's timing.

We must anchor our hope in that promise. We must set the hook of our faith firmly into the purpose God has shown us, and we must keep reeling until we see it manifest in our lives. Every crank of the reel brings the promise a little closer. Every "meanwhile" moment that passes, every lesson we learn, and every task we complete, brings us closer to reaching our full potential in God.

Great Cloud of Witnesses

The Bible is replete with heroes of the faith, such as those mentioned in the last section. Each of these men and women was just that—men and women. They had the same flesh we have, the same desires and failings. However, we're more than fleshly humans; we're supernatural children of the most high God. These heroes of the faith have something that sets them apart. They fulfilled the higher calling of God in their lives. They stand before us as a great cloud of witnesses to testify that we can also accomplish our destiny in God.

As we read stories of these heroes, we envision them with awe and reverence. These larger-than-life men are built up in our imaginations, and we feel certain we could never compare to their greatness. However, if we examine them closely, not as the heroes they became but as the people they were prior to taking on God's calling, we see a different picture of who they actually were. They were ordinary people, like us.

Abraham was a liar. In Genesis 12 and Genesis 20, Abraham said Sarah not his wife but his sister. Not only was he a liar, but he also didn't even follow God's commandments to the fullest. In Genesis 12:1-3, God visited Abraham and told him to leave his country and his kindred and go to a land He would show him. The Book of Acts indicates Abraham took his father's house and headed toward Canaan but stopped and dwelt in a town called Haran, named after his brother. Abraham's intentions were to follow God's instructions, but along the journey, he took a detour, leading his father's house with him. This directly contradicted what God instructed him to do. He settled in a new town, miles from his destiny. God had to tell him to get moving again.

In another instance, Abraham and Sarah tried to help God out by having a child with a surrogate mother. Even though God told them Abraham would father the baby with Sarah, they took it into their own hands to bring God's will to pass. What a mess that has been ever since. From the birth of this son came many tribes that warred against the nation of Israel throughout its history. The Islamic religion lays claim to the lands of the nation of Israel because they claim to be descendants of Ismael, Abraham's firstborn son through Hagar, Sarah's handmaid.

When we view Abraham from this perspective, we see a different picture. He was a liar. He was disobedient. He was hesitant. He placed himself above God by trying to take matters into his own hands. We've attempted many of the same actions in our own lives and callings. Even with all of these missteps, Abraham's faith was regarded as righteous.

There are many other witnesses in the Bible that serve as similar examples. King David was an adulterous, lying, murderous thief. Yet with all these failings, the Bible describes him as a man after God's own heart. It was not his fall that defined David; it was his repentant heart and determination to return back to God's call on his life that defined David's greatness. No matter what we face or how far we fall from grace, if we turn our hearts toward the call on our lives and pursue it with unwavering determination, God will bring it to pass.

In today's world, there are many witnesses to the potential God has placed within His children. People have overcome heinous and horrendous pasts by shifting their focus to the purpose God has placed within them. Time and pen could never document all the testimonies of people God has used to fulfill his master plan. Around each of us is a growing cloud of witnesses who can stand and testify to God's grace, mercy, and purpose in their lives. They can share how God took the remnants of a wasted life, regenerated it with Kingdom purpose, and called out the greatness within them.

We are without excuse. The miraculous power of regeneration is able to fulfill Godly purpose and calling. The lives of those who have allowed God to have His perfect will in their lives will stand either as encouraging testimonies or will stand as a testimony against us in the Day of Judgment. Step out on the faith of God's calling on your life and run! As you run, talk to those who have run before you. Read about those who have overcome countless obstacles to fulfill God's purpose. You can make it. You can fulfill your destiny in Christ. You can fulfill all the righteousness God has placed within you.

Don't Just Settle

Some people are settlers. They become complacent in their lives, mimicking what they have seen from their parents: uninspiring jobs, little education, small income—no purpose. They don't want to be seen as people who live above their social status, and they believe the lies of the generations before them.

"Ain't no one in our family ever got a college education, so don't get your hopes up that you'll ever get one. Our family has always been poor, but that's our lot in life. You've just got to make the best of it. We're just trailer trash. That is all people will ever think when they see you."

The Bible has much to say about who we are. However, many people let the world define them instead of choosing to believe God. They settle for a life molded by the words of others. Sometimes people look at the circumstances of their lives and accept the situation as permanent. The truth is, whatever God says you are is what you are. If He said, "I've made you more than a conqueror," then He has made you more than a conqueror. In your weakness, God's strength can be revealed.

A child of God is not a settler. We aren't born into His Kingdom to settle into the world. We're citizens of Heaven, born into the world to rule it. We're to transform it into the image of the Kingdom of God and to manifest His righteousness and glory. We can't afford to settle. The things of the world that we might consider accepting in no way compare to the riches afforded to us as children of God.

The world says we should be satisfied with our lot in life—our nice little house, our new automobile, our steady job. The Kingdom truth is that none of these material possessions provide satisfaction. These things belong to God and are entrusted to our care to be used for Kingdom work. These little luxuries should not lull us into a sense of contentment and satisfaction, which could lead to complacency. While we may enjoy these material blessings, true contentment only comes from fulfilling the calling of God on our life. This calling has nothing to do with materialism but everything to do with investing in eternity.

Our earthly circumstances do not define us. Our wealth or poverty is not our benchmark. We aren't measured by the standards of the world but by the stature of Christ. While the prosperity of life is alluring, the eternal reward for a life lived with Godly purpose is priceless. If we seek Him first, He will withhold no good things from us. He will provide our needs and supply the desires of our hearts. We cannot afford to settle.

Dwell on the Future, Not the Past

People love to dwell on the past and reminisce about the way things used to be. Nostalgia is a very powerful force. Over time, memories become softened and the truth hazy. For all its glory, the truth of past events is not nearly as glowing as the telling of it.

As we grow older, we have more in our past to remember. Storytelling has always been part of human culture. It's a way to pass down legacies and ensure our history and life lessons are not forgotten. It was the method selected by God to preserve the history of His people and the narrative of salvation through Jesus Christ. The true purpose of history is not to relive the past but to learn from it and live in the present with wisdom, knowledge, and understanding.

Many great movements have taken place throughout history. When we read about the men and women of God who were instrumental in initiating these movements, it's inspiring. However, if we dwell too much on these movements, they can become monuments and our focus shifts from the present to the past. There is no life in a monument, but movements are alive and active.

Many of the Christian Denominations can be traced back to a mover of God. For instance, John Wesley had an amazing encounter with God which sparked an amazing awakening. After his death, the Methodist and Wesleyan church denominations were formed as a testimony to his ministry. Like most denominations, these now stand as monuments to the movement.

God didn't give us a regenerative nature for our lives to become a monument of the moment we were saved. Many people remember with great emotion when God rescued them from a life of sin. However, just like many historical moves of God, they build a monument and never move further.

God has regenerated us to be an active, thriving movement in the Kingdom of God.

Fixating on the past will not bring purpose to our lives. It's easy to stay in the past because we've lived it; it's comfortable. Talking about the future is more difficult because we're limited in our knowledge of what's to come. We must speak of the future God has for us by faith. We must step out of what's comfortable while stretching our mind and faith to envision the calling God has spoken to us. In the midst of all the hindrances that might come against this great future, we must prophesy and declare all God has intended for us.

When we begin to move toward the future, we must stretch ourselves. We must push back against the forces that try to keep us within the limits of our own understanding. We even use common sense to justify our inactivity.

I've always wondered where common sense and faith intersect. To this date, I haven't found the answer. When He directs my steps, it rarely makes sense to me. When I follow my own plan, it is often perfectly logical to my mind, but the outcome is off the mark. When we align our actions with God's directions, the supernatural occurs.

I've come to believe this is where God desires us to live—outside of our own logic and in total faith and trust in Him. If we were able to plan and direct the path leading to our destiny, then we would be able to assume all the credit. When we find ourselves in the middle of God's perfect intended purpose, and we can't logically explain how we arrived there, the only thing left to do is glorify God.

Often, people pass through our lives to serve as scaffolding while our purpose is constructed. This ancillary structure provides craftsmen a place to work as the new edifice is erected. Once finished, the scaffolding can be removed to reveal the beautiful new structure underneath.

Similarly, people may pass through our lives, supporting us to change and grow. When they're no longer part of our lives, the loss may be momentarily painful, but the spiritual change may be immense. Know that our greatness is not determined by the people we associate with but by the magnitude of the greatness God has deposited within us. Seasonal relationships call forth the potential for greatness.

Often, people from our past are simply a piece of our history and have nothing to do with our future. We can't fixate on reestablishing former relationships that don't foster the proper environment for spiritual growth. We mustn't allow the influence of others who choose to live in the past, stop us from fulfilling our future. We need to shake ourselves loose from past memories and people who aren't helpful in our spiritual journey.

A sense of urgency must arise within us, a motivating force compelling us to manifest our future. We can't be satisfied sitting in a metaphorical easy chair with a remote in our hand, watching reruns from our past. We are called to fulfill a greater purpose.

The Bible tells us we can rest once we've died. Now is not the time to relax; it is time to labor in the field of the Lord. The harvest is ripe before us. We have received our assignment from the Master and have been equipped with all the tools, traits, and authority needed to accomplish His goals.

We must be aware of the inner sphere of greatness God has placed within us, then nurture and cultivate this seed. We have an incredible future, which we have been called to by faith. Learning from our past, operating in the present, and dwelling in our future will birth this God-given greatness from within.

Chapter Five

Creating an Environment for Spiritual Health – Environmental Determinates of Optimal Growth

"But grow in grace, and in the knowledge of our Lord and Saviour Jesus Christ. To him be glory both now and for ever. Amen."
(2 Peter 3:18 [KJV]).

All of creation is designed to flourish within a select set of environmental parameters. A fish will not grow on land. A bird will not survive in the depths of the ocean. Fruit bats will not live in the Arctic region of the world where no fruit exists. All creatures, great and small, have an ecological niche in which they receive the proper nutrients and climate that allow them to grow into the full stature of their genetically encoded potential. Take any creature out of its proper environment, and it will never reach its full potential—or more tragically, it will die.

This truth holds in the development of a child of God. There's an optimal environment for a child of God to reach its maximum God-given potential. Negative influences on this environment are easily modified by adjusting the nurturing culture or by removing the developing child from these harmful factors.

Romania has suffered from the number of children abandoned or placed in institutions. In 1990, a group of researchers initiated a study in the Bucharest orphanage. They selected 136 babies and randomly assigned them to either stay in the institution or to be placed within a foster home. They followed these children for thirteen years and evaluated their brain development. They found that staying in an institution altered the structure and function of the brain, decreasing its gray matter. Also, children who weren't placed in foster homes had decreased white matter, lower EEG activity, and poor social skills.

Other studies have shown that children with nurturing mothers had hippocampal volumes ten percent larger than those in motherless environments. This region of the brain is thought to be the center of emotion, memory, learning, spatial memory, and navigation.

Research has even determined that a child in utero can be affected by environmental influences from the mother. Genes can be silenced, or the expression of various proteins can be altered by the maternal influence on the womb. The term used for this environmental influence on gene expression is epigenetics (Chen and Zhang 2011, Ungerer, Knezovich, et al. 2013).

As we can see from this modern research, humans have an optimal environment in which they thrive physically. Alter the nurturing environment of the womb or the home, remove the father or mother, or change the number of nutrients a child receives, and you will alter the development of the child. Even though the DNA is present to develop a child into its maximum potential, environmental influences can't be ignored (McLanahan, Tach et al. 2013, Simpson, Gibbs, et al. 2017, Dukes and Palm, 2019, Guidolin, Anderlini, et al. 2019).

Through the induction of epigenetics, an altered fetal phenotype can emerge simply by the impact of maternal nutrition or environmental influences on the mother. This influence is so strong that a child born to an obese mother has a higher risk of developing obesity and diabetes than a child born to a fit mother. It's been shown to even affect the risk of diabetes for the third generation (Hancock, Lawrence, et al. 2014, Wang, Min, et al. 2017, Dhana, Haines, et al. 2018).

As Christians, we have two genetic codes: one for the sinful old man and one given to us by God through the regeneration of our heart by His Spirit. We have the potential to express either of these genetic characteristics.

The difference between phenotype and genotype is presentation. A person can have two genetically coded traits, for example, one for red hair and one for brown hair. The brown hair is dominant over the red hair. The genotype is "brown and red," but the dominant trait will be expressed. The environment can alter the phenotype or the physical color of the person's hair, so brown can become red with the proper "hairstylist."

Even as born-again believers, we can give life to the traits of sin that were crucified with Christ. This is why we must die daily and crucify this flesh and its desires. Therefore, the trait that dominates our life is the one that is expressed. The spiritual environment in which we place ourselves determines the spiritual phenotype that manifests.

It's possible for us to express sin's genetic code, and we can put ourselves in an environment that allows us to appear spiritual even though we are still manifesting a sinful nature inwardly. This type of person may look righteous, but this is simply self-righteousness. Someday, the roots will show forth our true color. The only way to manifest righteousness is to be born again and have a true spiritual genetic transformation before placing ourselves in an optimal environment for spiritual growth, which ensures the old nature is not given life by our quenching the Spirit and feeding the desires of the flesh.

The overcrowded nature of the world's religious institutions doesn't generate the ideal environment for optimal spiritual growth and development. For spiritual growth, we need to interact directly with a nurturing mother and directly with our Heavenly Father.

Our mother is the church, not the system as a whole, but the individual members mentoring one another in a personal, life-giving manner. This body of believers, unified under the banner of the King and acting in synergy with His heart, was strategically designed to produce the optimal environment for growth. The biggest hurdle facing proper spiritual development today is the absence of time spent with the Father and suboptimal nurturing from the mother.

Many books have been written on church culture and structure as well as systems-based approaches to church growth and development. Although there is no complete formula for creating an ideal environment for Christian spiritual growth, every effort should be made to study, read, seek wise counsel, pray, experiment, and measure and apply as many techniques as possible to create a fostering environment in every aspect of the church as a body.

At the end of the day, it's not the systems but the individual personal connection with God that provides optimal growth. Although there will be mistakes along the road, the church can't become a stumbling block for spiritual development, and God requires that we do our part as individuals within the church, so He can do His. It must be noted that the most powerful means of nurturing is unconditional love.

Epigenetic Influences

It's widely accepted that the genetic characteristics of an offspring are housed within the DNA contributed by its mother and father. This statement holds true to some extent. There are limitations to our understanding of how the genetic code is fully manifested in offspring. We've discovered over the last few decades that there are factors outside of the genetic map that influences expressed characteristics in offspring.

Numerous studies have examined the potential environmental and sociological influences that may affect the phenotypic expression of traits in offspring. These phenotypic traits are the biochemical or observable physical characteristics of an organism, as determined by both environmental influences and genetic makeup (Cassidy and Morris 2002).

As opposed to genotypic traits, which are the genetic makeup of an organism. Which refers to a single trait, set of traits, or an entire complex of traits (Churchill 1974). In short, the genotype is the sum total of genes transmitted from parent to offspring. Moreover, the phenotype is the expressed or observable traits of an organism. The phenotypic traits are not necessarily the full manifestation of an organism's complete genetic potential.

There are a number of factors that influence the phenotypic expression of an organism. For the purpose of this section, we will call the factors that affect phenotypes "epigenetic influences." Epigenetics was defined by Robin Holliday as "the study of the mechanisms of temporal and spatial control of gene activity during the development of complex organisms"(Holliday 1990).

We can see that an organism's environment will have an epigenetic influence on the traits an organism expresses. There are two sources of these environmental pressures that affect the epigenetic expression of genes. These are external and internal stressors.

So how does epigenetics affect our new nature? The interplay between the environment, our spiritual genetic potential, and our physical, genetic potential are tightly intertwined. In his excellent books, "The Biology of Belief" (Lipton 2005) and "Spontaneous Evolution," cellular biologist Dr.

Bruce Lipton explains in-depth how emotions can regulate genetic expression. Dr. Lipton postulates that DNA doesn't hold the secret to life (Lipton and Bhaerman 2010).

How the mechanisms within your cells respond to environmental influence is a stronger predictor of genetic expression than the DNA itself. Cells contain receptors on their surface that respond to various external stimuli and signals. These receptors send signals to the nucleus of the cell to turn on or off the production of genes, which then allows the cell to select a certain genetic blueprint based on the external environment.

Many of these cell receptors are regulated by chemicals that are secreted by the brain. Emotions are often responsible for these signaling molecules. These emotionally linked signaling events within our body will give rise to the type of genetic potential expressed. Even if we have the optimal genetic potential, our environment will determine the extent of the manifestation of that genetic potential.

The Bible simplifies this concept of emotionally linked genetic expression in Proverbs. The way we think in our hearts affects our physical being.

> *"For as he thinketh in his heart, so is he: Eat and drink, saith he to thee; but his heart is not with thee."*
>
> (Proverbs 23:7 [KJV])

The soul is the seat of our eternal identity. Our thought patterns set the tone of the environment that affects our spiritual DNA in addition to our physical DNA. Our genetic information doesn't have to be fully expressed. It can lay dormant. Our genetic potential rests within us, awaiting a signal to manifest.

Our perceptions, thoughts, and attitudes create the internal environment which influences the expression of our genetic blueprint. We must understand that our thoughts do not only affect our actions—they directly influence the expression of our full potential.

We are able to think about what we think about. We're able to evaluate our thought patterns and choose our emotional responses. We must no longer act as creatures who respond to environmental influence without thought. We have control over what we think about. We can think before we speak. We can evaluate our response before we express our emotions. We can control our internal emotional environment.

We no longer are driven by the thoughtless response of our fleshly nature. We've been given the power to live above it. To the point, we can directly influence our fleshly genetic expression by altering our emotional response to situations. By responding with our new nature, we initiate an internal signaling cascade that will display the physical manifestation of our new spiritual stature.

We must also be aware that the external stimuli we subject ourselves to are within our power to regulate. The friends we select, the conversations we choose to participate in, and the culture we choose to associate with all act as external stimuli that can alter our genetic expression.

In regard to epigenetic influences, our thoughts are not the only variable at play. There is a myriad of environmental influences, both internal and external, that can alter our genetic expression.

Nutrition

We need to understand the importance of nutrition in regard to our spiritual genetic potential. Nutrients are taken into the body and absorbed when we eat. In the spiritual sense, we must take in the Word of God, which is the bread of life, and digest it. This digestive process allows the nutrients found within the Word to be fully absorbed by our spirit, where they become life and strength to our inward man.

If we aren't receiving the Word, we won't grow spiritually. We need to make the Word of God a daily part of our spiritual diet. Lack of nutrition will stunt development, and in the case of severe malnutrition, it can lead to death.

The absence of nutrition removes the building blocks required for the production of proteins within the human body. Nutrients are required to express genetic potential. If we don't place our new nature within an environment where spiritual nutrients are available, we'll lack the resources required to manifest our new nature's characteristics.

It's our responsibility to place our new nature in an environment where it can obtain the required nutrients for optimal growth. As the old saying goes, "You are what you eat." What spiritual food are you feeding your soul? Are you placing yourself within an environment where the Word of God is taught and preached in a way that provides optimal nourishment, or are you content with just the milk of the preached Word? Are you actively engaged in reading and studying the Word of God, or have you allowed your Bible to become a trophy displayed upon the shelf? Are you actively seeking the presence of God daily in prayer and meditation? Are you meditating on the Word or simply hearing it and not applying it?

Proper nourishment requires both internal and external contributions. You can feed a child with a digestive disorder until his stomach distends. However, the food will lay useless within his body until he's provided the medicine required to break down the food and convert it into useable nourishment.

The same is true with the Word of God. We can sit in every church service every time the doors are opened. We can read the Bible from cover to cover every year. But until we begin to meditate and process the Word, our inward being will never provide our new nature with the nutrients it needs to manifest the full potential of our spiritual genetics. It's our responsibility to ensure we place our new nature in the proper environment.

Infections and Infestations

In many nations, illness due to infections and infestations of parasites and other opportunistic organisms are a major concern. Such infections and infestations have a direct effect on the person suffering. Most parasites carry medical risks that go beyond the area they are infesting. Many parasites compete for the nutrients the human host has eaten. In such cases, the secondary problem is malnourishment.

With opportunistic organisms such as bacteria and viruses, the physiological consequences are numerous. In severe cases, the infection can result in an immune response that can lead to death. However, many of these organisms have a symbiotic relationship with us. Sometimes these organisms are required to maintain our health.

For instance, within the digestive tract, there is a mixture of bacteria that aid in breaking down food. When a single organism becomes out of balance with the other, problems can arise. In such a case, the organism which has unchecked growth begins to consume all the resources that other organisms require to maintain their health. The problem is exacerbated when this organism kills off all the competition. With our bodies, bacteria can replicate to a point where their presence is detrimental.

Our spiritual nature is subject to both infection and infestations as well. These can come from both external and internal sources.

Internal sources of infection are similar in outcome to external influences. However, these infections come from within ourselves. We can begin a task in our lives that is not outside the realm of our destiny. However, this task can begin to consume our time and energy, causing us to lose sight of the overall picture that encompasses our calling.

These projects or activities may be a part of our perceived duty; they may actually play a vital role in the overall functioning of our God-given design. However, they're not the primary focus. We shouldn't place our full attention on areas of our destiny that can rob us of the time we need to dedicate to other aspects of our spiritual growth.

For instance, we can spend hours preparing a message for a service we're to speak at but fail to take time to pray. We can spend hours visiting the sick and never read the Word. We can minister to everyone in the community and never take time to minister to our own wife and children at home.

As with the external influence of infections, we must intentionally evaluate our priorities to ensure we're properly putting effort into what will produce the optimal environment for our spiritual growth. We can't allow one task or project to overshadow our destiny. In some instances, the project or task maybe someone else's destiny, and by not facilitating the transfer of responsibility to that person, we limit his ability to mature. Perhaps some tasks are better delegated than prioritized.

Everything we spend our time, resources, and energy on must be maximized if we're to reach our full potential. Only we can control the internal influences in our lives.

Internal sources of infestation are projects and tasks that have no bearing on our spiritual purpose. We can become consumed with tasks and projects that are simply time sinks. We can devote countless hours memorizing football facts when that time could be devoted to memorizing God's Word. We can dedicate countless hours to shopping for the best deal on the latest trends and neglect the person behind the register or with us in the clothing aisle that is hurting and in need of a life-changing word.

External sources of infections arise from the people with whom we associate. We're required as the children of God to interact with the world. The people of the world are our assignments. We need to interact with them to fulfill our Godly mission. However, there are people that influence our spiritual nature in such a way that they consume our time and resources to the point that we can no longer schedule time to fulfill our God-given purpose.

If we allow these external factors to consume our resources, it will result in a detrimental outcome to our spiritual development. We must evaluate our circle of influence and take the time to schedule our lives in such a way that we prioritize the tasks that produce the optimal environment for our spiritual nature. We must properly allocate the time needed for ministering to those whom God has placed in our lives. We only have a given amount of time in our life to fulfill our spiritual destiny. We can't afford to let parasitic people drain us of our most valuable limited resource—our time.

We must be cognizant of the fact that these people are opportunistic. They look for things that are going well in our spiritual life, and they come along for the ride. They glean the benefits of a relationship with us, but before too long, we begin to realize they are using us. Moreover, they consume time we could devote to others who are in need.

In such instances, we must take measures to limit the amount of resources we devote to these people to ensure we are ministering to others. If this is not addressed, these individuals will become detrimental to our ministerial efforts, and others within our care will suffer. We can actually allow their external influence to cause us to destroy ourselves.

Some external sources of infestation are people who consume our time and resources that are not a part of our normal circle of influence. God places us within other people's lives to serve a purpose and to manifest His presence. However, in the case of a person who is infesting our life, these people are not necessarily our circle of influence. These people are parasites looking to attach themselves to our lives and feast upon us until we can no longer support their insatiable appetite. Then they are off to the next host who will support them.

The result of a parasitic infestation is that it weakens or kills the host. We must be vigilant in order to identify people who become parasites. We need to evaluate our personal relationships and what we spend our time on. If these things do drain our spiritual nature, we need to determine if they are a parasite. They will zap the strength right out of us. The only way to deal with a parasitic infestation is to remove the parasite from our life.

There is also the risk that acquaintances from our past can latch onto us and draw us back into the old life we once lived. Sometimes these people can be reintroduced because we desire to encourage their spiritual growth. We may start hanging out with them to be a positive influence. Caution must be taken in these instances. We must protect our spiritual nature above all.

In most instances, it's best to introduce your old acquaintance to someone who can minister to them without the baggage of a past relationship. The possibility exists that the past relationship we had with the person can become an infection in our lives.

With regard to infections and infestations in our spiritual nature, the greatest key is assessment and prioritization. If we live a life that doesn't involve numbering our days, we aren't placing our new nature within an ideal environment for optimal spiritual growth.

Our top priority should be finding time to meditate on God in a secret place where we can find His guidance, knowledge, understanding, and wisdom.

Trauma

There are traumatic events that happen in everyone's life. Some trauma can leave people dismembered and suffering from debilitating injuries. Just as in nature, there are actions that can result in a traumatic spiritual event. Some of these are external, and some are internal. We may have found ourselves as the target of someone's wrath when it wasn't warranted. We may have been spoken to or judged by someone we felt was in authority over our spiritual wellbeing. There are numerous areas from which a traumatic spiritual event can arise. These events can leave a detrimental scar upon our new nature.

We must be aware that "hurt people hurt people." We may feel as if we can never overcome the debilitating events that have occurred. We may feel like our trauma is unsurpassable. Nevertheless, God has provided a wonderful tool to heal every traumatic spiritual event we've ever gone through. That tool is forgiveness. We must forgive for healing to begin in our spiritual selves. If we hold on to the hurt, we're placing our spiritual nature in the wrong environment.

We can't control the actions of others, but we can control our response. When we're faced with an event that causes spiritual trauma, we must forgive.

Internal and external traumas are much the same; the only difference is where the trauma originated. There are things we do that may traumatize our own lives. We may have really messed up in the past. There may even be haunting remnants of past sins that we're unable to remove from our lives. Some of these sins may predate our regeneration, and others may have occurred afterward. No matter the source of the trauma, it can have a negative influence on our spiritual nature.

It's hard to deal with internal trauma. We can waste countless hours rehearsing events repeatedly in our minds. We can go through a grieving process. We can look at what our future could have been without the trauma as if it's caused us to lose our destiny. We can try to justify it. We can try to rationalize it. We can try to look for an external cause. We can try to look for a new future and purpose through the lens of the trauma. However, nothing can fix the damage caused by internal trauma except for God. We must ask for forgiveness from God. Then comes the hard part: we must accept our own forgiveness. That's right; we must forgive ourselves. We can't justify what we did, but we can choose to forgive ourselves, so we can begin to heal and grow spiritually again.

It won't remove the potential ramifications of the trauma. Nevertheless, the trauma doesn't destroy our destiny. It can serve as a great instrument of humility that helps us realize we didn't choose ourselves—God chose us. When we finally reach the point of forgiveness, we're operating within the purpose God has designed for us; we can look back and know we didn't bring this to pass. God's grace and mercy brought us through, and He has established our position in Him.

Environment

I remember working as a bakery mechanic when I was in my 20's. I had worked with the construction company that had built the addition onto the bakery and was asked to come on board as a mechanic. The pay was good, but the schedule and environment were not. I was working 60 to 70 hours a week and going to college full-time. When I was hired, they told me they would pay for tuition. After school had started, they told me they would only pay tuition if it was a trade school. My time was so limited I was sleeping in my truck in the parking lot and trying to do my school work on my breaks. Going to church was almost impossible.

Something had to change. I remember talking to one of the production personnel about missing church. He was a former pastor. When he was hired, the company had told him they would give him Sundays off. This never happened, and he was forced to resign as pastor from his church because he needed the income.

After this conversation, I made up my mind my walk with God was more important than the income and stability this company had promised. I made a choice to leave this job. To this day, I would not change that choice

The environment we choose to spend our time within directly affects our spiritual nature and the ability of our new nature to access the requirements for growth. If we choose to place our spiritual nature in a job setting that limits our access to gathering with God's family, we'll lack the proper social influences required for optimal growth. If we choose to place ourselves in a group of people that cater to our old nature, we'll impoverish our new nature.

The internal stress of our environment is much the same; however, this stress deals more with where we allow our mind to dwell. If we allow our minds to focus on our past, our sins, and our regrets, we'll rob our new nature of its future. If we view the position of our new nature as socially and economically poor, our new nature will never develop. Our view of our spiritual nature must be through the eyes of faith. If we can't see beyond our current level of immaturity to the great potential and destiny God has for us, we'll never grow to embody our destiny.

The key to overcoming environmental stress is spending our time in the right places, both physically and mentally. We must select an environment that maximizes our growth. We must select friends that build us up and think on things that are vitreous. We aren't impoverished. We aren't socially challenged. We're the children of the most high God. We're the heirs to the wealth of this world. Our father owns the cattle on a thousand hills, and He will not withhold any good thing from us. So, we're without excuse if we select to place our new nature in an environment that is deprived.

Our control over the external climate related to the spiritual state of a region is limited to prayer. In some instances, we can have a direct effect by allowing God to lead us to elicit changes in the government or in politicians. The realm the enemy operates through is both corruptions in government policy and spiritual practices contrary to God's law. We must take a two-tier approach to combat these influences. We must pray to combat the Godless spiritual practices of our society and play an active role in putting Godly men and women within government offices.

Our external climate is, in some cases, difficult to change, but we must stay diligent in our efforts. However, if the change does not manifest, we don't have to be compliant with the climate of the world. We have the ability to set a different climate within the family of God.

The internal climate of the family is critical to our spiritual comfort. If we choose to sit in a cold house and not light a fire and we get sick, it is our own fault. The same can be said about the climate of a church family. If the church has gotten cold, we need to light a fire. We need to get back into the practice of seeking the fire of God within the family of God. Prayer and fasting are not suggestions for the family of God; they are climate changers.

If you want to turn up the thermostat, get a group of people together to pray. If you want the optimal spiritual environment in the family, you must have the fire of the Holy Ghost burning within the church.

We're called to be thermostats, not thermometers. We're called to adjust the spiritual climates of both our family and the world around us. If all we ever do is sit around measuring the spiritual temperature of the climate we're in, we'll never exercise our spiritual muscle and grow to reach our full potential. Our souls desire to be clothed with our heavenly dwelling. By regulating the climate around us, we can provide a heavenly environment in which our souls can flourish.

However, prayer can also warm up an environment literally! I remember reading years ago about a church in Europe during the seventeenth and eighteenth centuries that would warm their building from the heat of the men who would gather in prayer in the basement early in the morning.

Cultural Factors

Cultural factors sometimes are overlooked, but they're an influence that may affect growth. When you consider that some cultures regard certain foods and actions as taboo, it becomes more relevant to the discussion. For instance, some groups abstain from the consumption of meat. However, there are a number of amino acids, the building blocks of proteins present in meat, that are absent or at relatively low levels in a vegetarian diet. To offset this deficiency, alternative sources of amino acids must be supplemented in their diet. If a vegetarian doesn't get the proper nutrients, their growth—and health—may be stunted.

The same can be said about the spiritual culture in which we place our new nature. Cultural preferences don't have to be a bad thing. In some instances, cultural rituals are present due to perceived threats or personal comforts associated with the traditions.

I remember my Bible college days. The first-year students were not permitted to date for the first semester. They were only given one date, the second semester, and it had to be approved by the school. I thought this to be funny at the time. There were a number of other restrictions to male and female student interaction. One of which was you could not stay in a parked car with a member of the opposite sex.

I remembered a number of instances where couples allowed themselves the liberty to break these rules. Some without consequence other were not so lucky. Their desire to break these rules resulted in their desire for each other leading them to engage in activities God intended for marriage.

In retrospect, I can see the wisdom in these traditions to help those who are week in the faith or in the flesh from falling into sin.

Care must be taken, however, to ensure all resources required for our spiritual development are supplied even in the presence of cultural expectations.

For example, certain cultural pressures are more favorable than others regarding an individual's proper growth. There are warring tribes in various locations in Africa. It's their culture to be violent, but this expectation comes at a great cost to everyone involved. However, there are other societies, such as the Amish, who have cultural practices that not only benefit their own society but others as well. They may not drive cars or use electricity, but their skillset in agriculture and construction put them in high demand in the community.

In the context of our spiritual nature, there are two sources of cultural influence: those in society and those within our own lives.

External cultural influences will pressure us to conform to the sinful culture of society. These are detrimental to the health of our new nature. In some instances, these cultural traditions may pose no detrimental effect on our spiritual nature. We may hold the view while still maintaining our belief system. For instance, the social culture has changed regarding clothing style over the years. Men and women once wore robes, today there are a wide variety of outfits that people wear, and many vary based on the country the person lives in. Most clothing is modest for both males and females. The changing styles within a culture's clothing, as long as they remain modest, offer no impact on a person's spiritual nature. However, if the style introduced lascivious desires or immodesty, these must be avoided.

In some instances, cultural pressures may lead to the acceptance of underlying beliefs that can have dire consequences. For example, cultural expectations ask that we work hard, do our best, and strive to move up the corporate ladder. However, this cultural pressure has an underlying belief system: you must succeed at all costs, and your career takes priority over your family and God. Cultural influences can't be accepted haphazardly. Cultural pressure must be spiritually interrogated before we allow it to become a part of our new nature.

The internal sources of cultural pressure are our church and our own personal traditions. In some instances, various churches and denominations hold traditions that have carried on for years. We may often feel at home within these customs. At the time they began, they served a purpose, and they may still hold a great deal of sentimental value. These traditions are not necessarily bad, but it's possible to forsake spiritual growth if we're too caught up in them. In these cases, the tradition must be examined for its potential effect on the spiritual climate within its culture.

Secondary pressures are the cultural traditions that we hold within ourselves. We may often find we don't know where many of our beliefs and ideas come from. Some of us may have brought worldly traditions into our new life. Others may have maintained a perception of religion from when we were a child. In all instances, we need to examine our cultural viewpoint to determine if holding on to certain beliefs is in the best interest of our spiritual wellbeing.

We must also be sensitive to others' cultures. We can't allow our freedom from cultural tradition to negatively affect those who hold to tradition. For example, a singer was once asked to perform with a choir in a holiness church. When the singer arrived, she was wearing earrings. As she was preparing before the service, one of the ministers politely informed her the church preached against earrings. She graciously removed her earrings and sang with the choir.

In some instances, one individual's cultural pressures may differ from another individual's. I knew a man who didn't believe that a deck of cards should be in anyone's home. He believed it was a sin. From his perspective, it made perfect sense. He was a former gambler and had a very bad addiction before the Lord converted him, so the man's cultural tradition was to not have cards. However, by applying his tradition to the lives of others, he put undue cultural pressure upon those who didn't have the same weakness. To the point, he preached that if you had a deck of cards in your home, you were going to hell. He made no distinction between "Old Maid" or a poker deck; to him, they were all sin.

We are called to establish the culture of the Kingdom of God. We're tasked with changing the culture in the world we live in and in our homes. Understanding the dynamics of the culture of the Kingdom is vital to the maturation of our new nature. We can sometimes be so focused on the culture of the world or the culture of the church that we neglect to understand the culture of the Kingdom. The Kingdom of God is peace, love, and joy in the Holy Ghost. If we are to truly establish the culture of the Kingdom, we must do so under the Holy Ghost's lead.

Emotional Factors

We talked about the way emotions can affect our body's microenvironment. However, learning the origin of the influences that elicit emotional factors within our lives is as important as understanding their effect on our nature.

Emotions are difficult to explain. We all have them. We all express them in different ways. The method in which emotions manifest can come from two sources: external stimuli or internal stimuli.

From the time we're born and begin to interact with the world around us, we start to develop response patterns to external stimuli. In many cases, these responses are defined by emotional expression. For instance, if you find one hundred dollars in your pocket, you express joy. If your car gets hit in a parking lot, you express anger.

These emotional response patterns can be beneficial or detrimental to our spiritual health. We must examine why we respond the way we do. We must verify if the response pattern is appropriate for a child of God and if it is the most beneficial to our spiritual health.

There are also internal expression patterns. When we think someone is gossiping about us, we shun him. When we think someone is planning a surprise for us, we try to be overly friendly. When we allow our perception to determine our response, our behavior patterns need to be examined. We should look to the Word to determine the emotional response that best fits the situation. A passage from the Book of James does just that.

"My brethren, count it all joy when ye fall into divers temptations;."
(James 1:2 [KJV]).

Expressing joy in the middle of a trial is counterintuitive. Nevertheless, this is the scriptural basis for how to handle strife. We must understand the Word to determine the emotions we allow to influence our spiritual environment.

At the end of the day, our emotional expressions are the book the world reads. If we're a mess of emotional inconsistency and mayhem, what kind of story are we telling the world? We must gain control over our emotions and ensure we express what is the most beneficial to our spiritual health.

Emotions are a powerful component of our physical and spiritual nature. It can be said that our emotions serve as a bridge whereby our internal nature expresses itself to the world. We can either allow our emotions to be driven by our flesh or allow them to be controlled by our spirit. The sources of emotional control are a good measure of an individual's spiritual maturity. If the flesh drives our emotions, we need to examine our walk and assess our spiritual health.

Chronic Diseases

Chronic disease is a debilitating stress upon development. Children who suffer from chronic illness are limited in their growth. Utilizing resources to fight off chronic infections robs the body of its ability to use nutritional resources for growth.

For our spirit, sin is the most detrimental and chronic disease. In our new nature, there are two sources of sin. There are the sins of others and our own sins.

The influence of others' sins can rob us of time, resources, energy, sleep, and soundness of mind. When our children or loved ones are living in sin, we can spend a great deal of our spiritual lives worrying about them. It is only natural that our prayers and our concerns for them are at the forefront of our minds. Nevertheless, we can't stop them from sinning. It may cause us heartbreak, but the only weapon we have is prayer and love. We must love them in the midst of their mess. However, we can't be so overcome with grief that it robs us of the time we need to devote to our own spiritual development and ministry.

The internal influences of sin are more difficult to manage. In truth, many people have hidden sins or areas of weakness and refuse to address them. In some instances, we're embarrassed to seek help. In other instances, our guilt overpowers us. The devil tries to convince us that we are alone in our sin or no one will understand. However, the truth is we are not alone. Many people have walked down the same road, and they're willing to offer guidance and counsel to help us overcome our own mess.

Nine out of ten Christian men say pornography is a factor that inhibits their relationship with God. One out of seven people is in debt, which is detrimental to their financial wellbeing. Sin doesn't show favorites. However, internalized sin can isolate us from help. We must find good counsel and support in God's family, who can help us move beyond our personal sin. If our sins have become chronic, they're not beyond God's grace and mercy. However, they may require us to die to ourselves and let others assist us. Our spiritual health and growth are dependent upon it.

Sin is like cancer. If we allow it to continue to grow, it will quickly invade every part of our spiritual nature. We'll begin to struggle to keep hope and faith alive in our lives. Before long, sin will destroy our relationship with God and others. Finally, sin will kill us. We must find the cure for sin in our spiritual nature. That cure is Jesus.

Ordinal Position in the Family

This is an odd concept, but, in some cases, our perception of birthright can affect our spiritual growth. Within the context of some animal families, this is of great importance. When you are the smallest of your siblings, you may struggle to get to the food. However, this is not so in the family of God.

I have often seen a distorted concept of honoring those who are elders. In such cases, the elder takes an authoritative role over the one who is younger or weaker in the faith and dictates the actions and behaviors of the younger person. This should not be so in the Kingdom of God. The elder should be lifting the younger upon his shoulders to heights he himself has never been.

The pressure of perceived birth order in the church can cause stunted growth in the youth and will prevent the elders from maturing. Everyone is born into the Kingdom of God with a unique set of skills and a specific God-given purpose. When an older person in the faith takes on a position mandating the actions of a child of God, they have stepped out of their role. Instead, the elder is expected to lead the child to a deeper relationship with God, where the child can discover how his specific skills and talents can be maximized. The authoritarian role is contrary to the teaching of Christ.

> *And he said unto them, "The kings of the Gentiles exercise lordship over them; and they that exercise authority upon them are called benefactors. But ye shall not be so: but he that is greatest among you, let him be as the younger; and he that is chief, as he that doth serve. For whether is greater, he that sitteth at meat, or he that serveth? is not he that sitteth at meat? but I am among you as he that serveth.."*
> (Luke 22:25-27 [KJV])

There is no positional stress in the Kingdom of God. We're all fellow laborers, and we're here to lift each other up, not lord over each other as masters. We're to respect our elders and honor them, and elders must be aware of the detrimental effect they can have on those who are coming up behind them if they fail to operate according to the Biblical model.

We must consider that we all are in various stages of spiritual growth and development. There is always someone who is our elder and someone who is our junior. We must work together to build one another up as a family unit, iron sharpening iron. When we feel we are superior to others in the family, we must remember there's only one head in the household of faith, and that position belongs to Christ.

That being said, we must also remember to respect our elders and learn from them. In today's culture, many people have lost respect for those who have walked before them. This may be due to an elder's improper handling of his authority. Nevertheless, elders have a better view of the path that lies before us than any others. In a multitude of counselors, there is safety, so exercise wisdom and seek out the counsel of as many elders as will mentor you.

If we're the elders, we must seek to serve the youth with honor. We must mentor children as Christ served His disciples. There should be no jockeying for position or for power within the Kingdom of God.

Growth Potentials

Within a natural environment, the maximum growth potential of a person is coded within their genetics. If all variables are optimized and negative influences are removed, the only limiting factor is DNA.

The same is true in the family of God. We all are capable of greatness. The growth potential we have within our new nature is limitless. However, we often allow limitations to be placed upon our growth potential.

External factors affecting our growth come from the opinions and actions of others. Too often, we allow the words and treatment of those closest to us to alter our view of our own potential. In many instances, the view of a parent or person we respect sets the boundaries we place on our spiritual growth. Instead of listening to the Word of God, we allow the words of others to label us and define our identity and potential.

Internally, we know where we have fallen short. We know the areas where we struggle. We begin to see ourselves through the perspective of our shortcomings. God doesn't see these shortcomings. He is more than able to do away with temptation and make a way for our escape. We must trust in

His Spirit to lead us to the point of maturity so we can overcome the stumbling blocks in our lives.

We must grab hold of the truth of God's word. We must establish our faith in who He says we are and press on in faith until we become what He says we are. We must plant our faith and identity upon His perception of our growth potential. If we never see ourselves as the mature son or daughter God has destined us to be, we will never maximize the growth potential that lies within us.

Toxins

In nature, there are numerous environmental toxins that can adversely affect human growth. These toxins come from numerous sources and have different effects on the body. The main route of exposure to toxins is through oral ingestion. In some instances, toxins may have a nonlethal exposure limit. Others may have a dose range that humans can tolerate. Nevertheless, this range is very narrow, and exceeding it can have detrimental consequences.

The main route of spiritual toxins is through our minds. These toxins can either be self-administered or administered to us by others. Sources of toxic ingestion come from other people placing thoughts within our minds. Their thought patterns, their behaviors, their gossip, their murmuring, their complaining, and their spiritual environments affect our spiritual nature. These people are opportunistic in their approach, like a viper with toxic venom. In other instances, they are deliberate in their attempts to assassinate our spiritual nature, dumping their toxins into the church as a whole.

The opportunistic look for vulnerability, injecting a thought here and there until that toxin becomes the first thing you think of when you feel vulnerable. When the pastor doesn't shake your hand, the toxin says, "He doesn't really care. He only notices the rich people in the church." The toxin begins to pollute how you see everything.

Deliberate poisoners of toxins look for things that are going well or poorly in the church; they take ownership of the good and spread the blame for the bad. They inject their opinions and judgmental observations into everyone in the church. These thoughts then reside in our minds, slowly poisoning us as we give them our attention. Every time these people are around, they are rehearsing how they would change things or how they are the reason things are so excellent.

They plant toxic thoughts within your mind, then they hang around to apply a second dose. These thoughts, before long, elicit a response from within us, as factors in the environment are not going our way. The accumulation of these thoughts creates an internal response that isn't beneficial to our spiritual maturity. If left unchecked, this can result in spiritual death. We can actually allow these external influences to cause us to destroy ourselves. This is why the Scripture instructs us on the proper thoughts that we should meditate upon.

> *"Finally, brethren, whatsoever things are true, whatsoever things are honest, whatsoever things are just, whatsoever things are pure, whatsoever things are lovely, whatsoever things are of good report; if there be any virtue, and if there be any praise, think on these things."*
>
> (Philippians 4:8 [KJV]).

Internal sources of toxic exposure are similar in outcome to external influences. We may begin to entertain thoughts that aren't in agreement with our spiritual destiny. As we allow ourselves to think these thoughts over and over again, we may begin to look for evidence to support our negative thought patterns. Before too long, we'll find confirmation that supports these thoughts. If left unchallenged, they'll destroy our spiritual nature, not by the presence of the thought itself but by the fact we allowed the negative pattern to develop. This evolves into a preconditioned response within our spiritual nature that, when unleashed, creates collateral damage we can't escape.

We must be careful what thoughts we entertain. Whether these thoughts originate from external or internal sources, we need to evaluate them to ensure they aren't outside of our tolerance level for toxicity. We can and must examine our thoughts. We must meditate upon those things that are virtuous.

Producing the Optimal Environment

An optimal environment requires a consistent, directed effort on our part to obtain maximum spiritual growth. That said, we can't achieve it alone. The Holy Spirit lives within us to lead us and guide us into all truth. It's our comfort and teacher. Nevertheless, too often, we don't let the Holy Spirit do His perfect work in our lives.

The Spirit must lead us. We must ensure we place our new nature within an environment that eliminates negative influences on our spiritual genetic expression. We must ensure we give our new nature the optimal nutrients required for spiritual development. We must reduce and eliminate any infection or infestation that exists within our environment.

We can be delivered from chronic disease. We must seek healing for the trauma that we've experienced to ensure proper healing within our new nature. We must realize the limitless resources available to us through our heritage in the Kingdom. We must understand, we're the climate setters, not the world. We influence our culture. We manage our emotional response to stimuli.

We aren't subject to ordinal positions; we're all fellow laborers with Christ and have free access to the limitless provisions of Heaven. We can't allow ourselves, or anyone other than God, to dictate our growth potential. Moreover, we must free ourselves from negative thoughts that can kill our God-ordained dreams and destiny. As Children of God, we need to place ourselves in the proper environment and recognize the choices we make directly affect the process of our spiritual maturity.

We're a part of two environments: the environment that is created when we come together as the church and the environment we manifest when we are living out our daily lives.

We must intentionally develop a healthy environment in both locations. The environment created as we gather as the church is critical for the early development of a new convert. It serves as the womb to the newborn child of God, nurturing and protecting its development. This environment builds the traits needed to interact with the world.

The second environment in which we interact with the world also has a great influence on our spiritual health. We must not neglect the influence our behaviors have on a new convert. He will see our actions among men, so in all things, we must represent the Kingdom.

Given that this task has been placed in our care, how do we cultivate this environment? What tools has the Lord left us?

> *"All scripture is given by inspiration of God, and is profitable for doctrine, for reproof, for correction, for instruction in righteousness."*
>
> (2 Timothy 3:16 [KJV]).

God's Word has been given to us as a powerful tool to establish the environment of the Kingdom. It provides doctrine to instruct us in truth. This truth helps us combat toxic thoughts, such as a lack of the sense of right and wrong, doing whatever feels good, and many other lethal factors that influence a healthy spiritual environment.

The Word is a source of training and protection, and it provides the inner man with nutrients to grow. It convicts us of improper thoughts, actions, behaviors, and desires. The Word makes us aware of the heart of the Father. The Word straightens us out, corrects our trajectory, and puts us back on course.

The word, translated in the passage above as "instruction," is the Greek word *paideia*, which means to nurture and create an environment for growth and discipline. God has given us His Word to help us create the environment of His Kingdom.

There are three things we must take away from the content presented here. The first is we must realize the importance of the environment on a new convert's development. The second is we must understand we're responsible for ensuring this environment is maintained both within the context of the church and in our daily lives as we interact with the world. The third is we've been given the pattern and the necessary tools within God's Word to manifest this environment. We must step up to the task.

Chapter Six

Grow Up – Taking Ownership

"That ye might walk worthy of the Lord unto all pleasing, being fruitful in every good work, and increasing in the knowledge of God;."

(Colossians 1:10 [KJV]).

The first half of this book addressed many variables that function to assist us in understanding our new nature. Much of it has been descriptive, covering the mechanism and process of regeneration, in addition to the various factors and roles required to carry out the maturation process. It's been presented to reinforce the knowledge, understanding, and the fact that we have been given a new nature.

Now it's time to address the most critical component to the maturation process: the role you and I must take in ensuring we reach spiritual maturity. Everyone reading this book knows a child doesn't grow up alone. There are a number of influences on a child's maturation. Nevertheless, along the way, there are contributions that are strictly the child's responsibility. The child must take ownership of his actions and the consequences of those actions.

There comes a point in our lives where we must take ownership of our path. We must move from an infant through the various developmental stages to an adult. No one can do this for us; we must step up to the plate and do our part. However, we can't do this alone. We require some external help.

Our genes set the maximum level of our full potential, but the environment we place ourselves in establishes the limit to which this potential is manifested. Physical, emotional, spiritual, and psychological environments contribute to defining these limits.

Knowing how complex the process of development is, leaves us with the need to place the process within a defined set of steps. To better understand how and when various factors can have the greatest influence on our development, these steps must be demarcated. In this chapter, I've chosen to use a chart I fashioned after Erik Erikson's psychosocial stages model.

Stage	Crisis	Virtue	Question	Age
1	Trust vs. mistrust	Hope	Can I trust the Lord?	Infancy
2	Autonomy vs. shame	Will	Is it ok to be me?	Early childhood
3	Initiative vs. guilt	Purpose	Is it ok to for me to do, move, and act?	Play age
4	Industry vs. inferiority	Competency	Can I make it in the world of people and things?	School age
5	Ego identity vs. role confusion	Fidelity	Who am I? Who can I be?	Adolescence
6	Intimacy vs. isolation	Love	Can I love?	Young adult
7	Generativity vs. stagnation	Care	Can I make my life count?	Adult hood
8	Ego integrity vs. despair	Wisdom	Is it ok to have been me?	Maturity

Erikson's model outlined the concept that, at various points in one's life, specific virtues are developed. There are eight stages to the model, and we must look at each of these stages from three points of view. Using his hierarchy of stages, I have overlaid the stages of development within a child of God's life.

First, we must understand the stages from the standpoint of a child's natural maturation. This will set the context for our understanding. It'll also provide us with a clear picture of how this stage in development is important to ensure a child's healthy growth. Secondly, we'll view each of these stages from the standpoint of their environmental influences. Thirdly, we'll view them from the standpoint of our personal responsibility within each stage to ensure maximum potential is reached.

Hope

In Erikson's model, the stage of hope is defined by the conflict of "Trust vs. Mistrust." It's the time in children's lives when they learn to trust their needs will be met. For the infant, the constancy of a primary caregiver is vital to development. If infants aren't given the care required to meet their basic needs, they develop a sense of mistrust that can stay with them for the duration of their lives. Erikson defined this stage with the question, "Can I trust the World?" Infants have no choice but to depend on others to take care of them. If infants develop a sense of trust at this stage, they will attain the virtue of hope.

It's not hard to see the vital role this stage plays in the developmental process of a child. In the context of a child of God, this stage is just as important. When a soul first comes into a relationship with Christ, it must rely on someone for assistance. Infants of God don't know how to feed themselves or how to clean up the mess that is hanging around them from their old life. This is where the primary caregiver comes in.

God placed the church in the role of the mother to help nurture the infants who are born into the Kingdom. They need to have their needs met. At times, we may know what those needs are. However, there are times we know there's a need but are clueless as to what will satisfy it. As members of the church, we must take up the task of caring for these newborn babies, help them clean up after themselves, help feed them, nurture and soothe them when they cry, and love them. Most of all, we must pray for them and for the wisdom to discern what they require.

There will come a time when they're in need of something that will test their faith. This is a vital time in the development of a child of God. We, as the church, need to be sensitive to the voice of God in these moments. God's child may have a financial need. The Lord may speak to us to give him money. He may need some food in his home. The Lord may place it on our hearts to drop by with some groceries. He may just need words of encouragement. Our sensitivity to the voice of God at these times is vital in guiding us to speak in his life to develop hope.

These children can't take care of developing these aspects of their faith on their own. We must, as a church, step up to the plate and take on our role as the primary caregiver.

Many people aren't at a stage in their development to become a primary caregiver to an immature child of God. However, each of us can look back and reflect on this time in our lives. Many of us may have failed to successfully navigate this stage. Nevertheless, hope is not lost. If you put your trust in God, He will stimulate hope again in your life.

In the context of the family of God, the most pertinent question for this stage is, "Can I trust the Lord?" or "Can I trust the church?"

Many of us, if we're honest with ourselves, will agree our answer to this question is tempered. "Kind of? Sometimes? Depends on what I'm trusting Him for." Most Christians don't successfully navigate this stage.

What can we do if we realize we were unsuccessful at moving past this stage in our walk with God? What if our spiritual life is filled with a lack of trust?

The first thing we must do is acknowledge that we need to develop a greater sense of trust in God. Identifying the areas in our past that have led to distrust can be helpful. The best approach is to seek God and let Him help walk us through the development of our hope.

> *"Therefore being justified by faith, we have peace with God through our Lord Jesus Christ: By whom also we have access by faith into this grace wherein we stand, and rejoice in hope of the glory of God. And not only so, but we glory in tribulations also: knowing that tribulation worketh patience; And patience, experience; and experience, hope: And hope maketh not ashamed; because the love of God is shed abroad in our hearts by the Holy Ghost which is given unto us."*
>
> (Romans 5:1-5 [KJV])

As we mature in this stage of our spiritual life, we'll be faced with suffering. Nevertheless, through this time of tribulation, we'll begin to develop patience and fortitude, which will sustain us through our development. This fortitude will ripen our Godly character—the traits and characteristics that we were given to us through the process of regeneration. The development of these characteristics will establish our hope in God.

If we're at this stage, what steps can we take to ensure we're successful? The answer is to trust God. There is no way to mature without doing so. God uses people to fulfill His will and His plan, but people are often disobedient. If you find yourself experiencing this in your Christian walk, don't let the lack of a caregiver define or destroy your confidence in God.

You're going to face times of need and distress. These trials aren't meant to destroy you; they're meant to build your character. Growing is a painful process. There are unpleasant changes in the natural body that take place, but they're required for proper development. If you are at this point of your spiritual maturity, rest assured this is only a brief season in your development. It will pass. You will grow and move to the next level. It may seem overwhelming, and it may look like there's no hope in sight. Nevertheless, the struggle is required for our development.

As an infant passes through this stage of its life, it struggles. It struggles against the aspects of gravity. It struggles against the need for attention and how to obtain it. It struggles against the need to have its diaper changed. All these struggles are required. As the baby moves its body against the forces of gravity, it strengthens its muscles. As a baby cries to get attention, it develops its lungs. As a baby struggles with its bodily waste, it learns to control those functions. Without these struggles, the simplest of tasks would never be mastered.

If it feels like you're never going to make it, if it feels like there's no hope, be patient; it's on its way.

> *"Hope deferred maketh the heart sick: but when the desire cometh, it is a tree of life."*
>
> (Proverbs *13:12* [KJV]).

Will

The second stage of psychosocial development laid out by Erikson is autonomy versus shame. This stage is defined by the existential question, "Is it OK to be me?"

During this time in children's lives, they're beginning to explore their world. They're gaining control over their motor abilities and interacting with their surroundings. Their parents provide a strong and secure base from which they can venture out and express their will. These children are constantly learning about their environment.

The first interest of a child begins to surface at this age—they begin to express their personality and talents. During this stage, the parent's approach can play a vital role in the child's progression and outcome. If a parent is overly restrictive, the child may develop a sense of doubt in himself or a reluctance to attempt new challenges.

If the caregiver refuses to let the child perform a task, demands too much too early, or ridicules the child's attempts, the child may develop self-doubt and shame. Encouraging self-sufficient behavior helps children develop autonomy. This autonomy allows children to identify and express their will in a positive and productive manner without doubt and shame.

As the church, we're given the task to encourage children of God through this stage in their spiritual development. The opportunity to express themselves as individuals helps define their identities. Exploring the environment around them and the various talents and skills that have been transferred to them through the regenerative act of God is vitally important to their maturation.

As the church, we can't stop them from trying, and we can't criticize them when they don't do something well. We can very easily take the motivation from the child by demanding they act in a way that is above their level of maturity. We must avoid taking an opportunity from them, doing tasks for them, or ridiculing them when they try.

If we ourselves are at this stage in our spiritual maturity, we must take inventory of how we may determine the limits of our environment.

What influence do I have?

Where can I make an impact?

What do I like to do?

What are my talents and skills?

During this time, we're exploring the will of God in our lives. We may not completely understand His leading, but it's during this time He will provide us the vision of our future that will sustain us through our faith's trials. It's in the midst of exploring the vastness of our new nature that we find the uniqueness that makes us His prized possession. We must come to realize we're His child with our own personality and means of contributing to His Kingdom.

We must not lose the desire to try. Even when others make fun of us or try to do things for us, we must try. We may fail and make mistakes, but that's a part of growing up. We need to surround ourselves with people who encourage self-sufficient behavior.

One danger to this time of development is our past. The mistakes of our past can cloud our thoughts. If we allow ourselves to entertain the thoughts, ways, and actions of our past, or if we allow the shame of our past mistakes to define what we can be in Christ, we'll become full of shame. We must not allow what we once were to prevent us from grasping onto the promise God has for our new life. We must, by faith, sink our affections into the hope of God's promise for our life.

Purpose

The third stage of psychosocial development laid out by Erikson is initiative versus guilt. This stage is defined by the existential question, "Is it OK for me to do, move, and act?"

At this stage in children's development, they are beginning to plan and attack a task just for the sake of being active. They're learning to master their environment, develop an understanding of the principles of physics and learn basic skills. They want to complete their own actions. They begin to develop a confusing sense of guilt when what they're trying to accomplish doesn't result in the desired outcome.

This period brings a sense of initiative and provides a feeling of security concerning their ability to make decisions and lead others. The child develops independence and courage. This stage can also be a time when unwanted behaviors begin to manifest. As a child experiences frustration at what they're unable to accomplish, they may engage in conduct that is inappropriate and aggressive.

At this time in a child's development, a parent needs to help the child set realistic goals for himself while helping him develop initiative and independence in planning activities. If the parent discourages independence and views the child's needs and desires as bothersome or silly, the child will develop guilt.

As a church, we must be willing to help our spiritual children who are maturing through this developmental stage. We need to interact with them in a way that helps them develop their understanding of God's principles by setting achievable goals for fulfilling a greater purpose. When these new children of God approach us with desires for independence and a wish to initiate a project, we must be sure to encourage this independence while helping them set realistic boundaries.

We can't afford to dismiss these children at this time in their spiritual development. If we dismiss their ideas as silly or bothersome or discourage their desire to lead and take the initiative, they'll begin to feel their autonomy is questioned, and their needs and desires will become a point of guilt.

This is also the time that you'll see outbursts, especially if their plans don't work out as designed. They'll blame the church, individuals in the church, God, and whomever they feel may have interfered. This is a great opportunity to take these children aside and examine what happened. These are teaching moments that will build a lasting foundation. However, it must be done correctly, and this, too, is a skill that must be developed within the church.

If we are at this stage in our spiritual maturity, we must understand others may not realize our zeal to step out and take the lead is motivated not by pride but by our desire to give legs to our autonomy and find our purpose. We're trying to take the initiative to manifest the characteristics we see within ourselves.

There will be people who make fun of our initiative and dismiss us as bothersome. Nevertheless, during this stage, we must learn how things operate in the Kingdom of God. We must learn the rules of the Kingdom, learn how to apply those rules to our actions, and learn how our actions produce results. These are vital to channeling our initiative without detrimental behaviors.

It's a great idea to take the time to find a mentor who can help you through this developmental stage—someone who can help you learn the principles of how God works and how to set realistic goals you can build upon to fulfill your God-given purpose.

Competency

The fourth stage of psychosocial development laid out by Erikson is industry versus inferiority. This stage is defined by the existential question, "Can I make it in the world of people and things?"

At this stage in their development, children feel the need to win approval by demonstrating specific skills or competencies, and it's their peers they turn to for that approval. When they receive encouragement and reinforcement, they'll feel confident and industrious, which inevitably bolsters their ability to accomplish goals and build self-confidence. This is a vital time in the developmental process because this is when a child begins to better understand their interests and recognize their special talents.

If this approval is not received, children begin to doubt their abilities and feel inferior, so they may not reach their full potential. If a child is not allowed to discover their talents in their own time, they'll lose motivation, become lethargic, and have low self-esteem.

When the children of God, who've been placed in our care, begin to transition to this stage of development, we need to become their greatest fan. As they hone their specific skills and talents, we need to make opportunities for them to display their gifts. We need to step up, give them the resources and support they require and help pair them with people who can help develop their talents.

Some talents may be outside of our depth of knowledge, so we must take the initiative to seek out ways in which these maturing Christians can grow. In the grand scheme of things, we must ensure they don't lose their motivation and instead develop confidence and self-esteem.

If we are at this stage in our spiritual maturity, we must know not everyone will understand our gifts and callings. Some may be jealous; others may not like change. There may be people who see you as who you once were or as too young, and they'll fail to put your talents to work. Nevertheless, the Bible assures us a person's gifts will make room for Him. Hone your skills and talents until the Lord gives you an opportunity.

We must be careful not to look to the world for approval. There is a very strong attraction to seeking the approval of the world, and we must protect ourselves. God gave our skills to us, and He has a perfect plan that will maximize the use of those talents and gifts.

We must seek the approval of God in the absence of the approval of others. If we ask God to provide us with wisdom and place us in an environment that will help develop our talents, He will make a way. He can direct us to someone who will assist us in becoming more competent.

Our overall motivation at this stage is to not step through the first door that opens to us. We must ensure that we hold tightly to God's will for our lives. Our gifts and callings will make room for us, but they can also fill the gaps left by those who haven't stepped up to do their part in the Kingdom of God. Therefore, as we mature through this stage, we must ensure we're following God's perfect will for our destiny and not the will of other men or our desires. We may be called upon to fill gaps others have left vacant, but you must never stop refining your gifts and pursuing your calling.

We must also take inventory of ourselves so we don't simply fill a vacancy. We must be dynamic and accept or turn down opportunities presented to us. Additionally, we must be flexible by following God into new endeavors and stepping aside from current plans to allow others room to grow. Sometimes God uses us as space fillers to occupy a role until the proper person can step into the position. These are great learning opportunities but aren't our final destination. Often people step into the first opportunity they're given and are there for life when God simply wanted to use the experience to mature them to fulfill a greater purpose. These people become unfulfilled, resentful, and may feel trapped.

To guard against these pitfalls, we must look back at our hope and stand firm in our calling. Never settle for less than God has promised you can become. Enjoy every step and count it as a learning experience that will get you to God's ultimate destiny. Know that God rejoices over every step you take toward your destiny.

Fidelity

The fifth stage of psychosocial development laid out by Erikson is identity versus role confusion. This stage is defined by the existential question, "Who am I, and what can I be?"

In the development of a child, this is a critical stage. At this point, the need for identity hasn't been met. The child has developed many forms of identification, but he hasn't developed a clear view of who he is. This is a time of transition from the early stages of development to the later stages—a transition from who a child was to what the child will become in his adult life.

The myriad of physiological changes and social changes make this a turbulent time for adolescence. As children transition, they must balance the questions, "What have I got?" and "What am I going to do with it?" This transition helps define their identity. They are coming to grips with their sexuality and all the emotions and hormonal changes associated with this period of their lives.

Because there are a number of voices trying to sway the perspectives of the adolescent, they're left feeling pulled in multiple directions, such as their internal wishes and the external opinions of peers, society, parents, etc. If a teenager experiences too much insistent pressure from his environment, he will "foreclose" on experimentation and true self-discovery. In such a setting, the reluctance to commit may haunt him into his adult life.

Given the proper space, time, and freedom to explore and experiment, a sense of deep and emotional awareness of who a child is will emerge. This emotional awareness will give rise to a firm sense of identity, and this emerging identity helps develop fidelity—a sense of loyalty, faithfulness, and devotion to one's self. The pressing question that must be answered internally in this child is, "What are my beliefs, feelings, and attitudes?"

As a church, we have children of God who are going through this stage in their spiritual life. It's not easy, nor is it pretty. They're struggling internally with who they are and who they are going to become. We can't force them to become what we think they should be. By forcing a child of God to be what we think they should be, we hinder him from fully developing his sense of identity.

A child of God without a secure identity is like candy to the devil. He is looking for these unstable Christians. They only do what they are told to do. They base their entire Christian walk on the approval of others, and when the trials come and the storms rage, they look for answers from their peers. They don't have enough internal fortitude to weather the storms of life. They don't know how to properly respond, and when they do, they don't know themselves well enough to understand why they responded to the events in such a way.

The internal conflict between who they are and what people want them to be can't be resolved. They're constantly seeking out advice from others, never maturing, and never growing up. They don't have a sense of who they truly are in Christ. They doubt their own callings and talents. They aren't loyal to their own internal morals. They'll say whatever the group likes to hear. When it comes to being faced with an opposing view, they'll follow the crowd.

This developmental stage requires a great deal of patience and love. They'll ask every question they can think of to uncover their own beliefs. At this point, it's not a good time to argue with them. Their questions, instead, pose great teaching moments. For every question they raise, give them the opportunity to do the homework. Tell them various views concerning their question, then have them study and give you their conclusion. This will help them better define their beliefs.

If we are at this stage in our spiritual maturity, we're struggling. We may begin questioning our faith. We question everything we've ever been told both within the church and outside of the church. Our faith is shaken, and we don't know who we really are anymore. We know we can't fulfill the calling God placed on our lives like this. We feel unprepared and ill-equipped.

You can't rationalize your feelings and your experience. You want to ask every question you can think of, and when people respond in a manner that is dismissive or accusative, your resolve to vocalize your point results in hostility.

At this time in our development, we need to do an internal assessment. We need to know who we are. We need to know what we have and what we are going to do with it. This will set the foundation upon which we can find stability, a place our confused state of mind can run to, and gain a fresh perspective. This foundation can only be found in the Word of God. It's at this time we must come to the revelation that we are who God says we are.

Love

The sixth stage of psychosocial development laid out by Erikson is intimacy versus isolation. This stage is defined by the existential question, "Can I love?"

At this developmental stage, a child has transitioned into adulthood; however, some unresolved issues may still persist. A latent period overlaps identity versus role confusion, which persists into this stage. Because of the overlap, there is still a driving force to blend in with friends. This desire to fit in sometimes imposes a growing desire for intimacy. Fear of rejection and the emotional pain associated with rejection can be more than one's ego can bear. In these instances, isolation is selected over the fear of rejection.

This isolation can culminate in negative behaviors toward others. These behaviors are driven by the motivation to destroy people who appear dangerous to their identity and who seem to be encroaching on their intimate relations.

If a healthy identity is established at this point in a person's life, he's ready to establish long-term commitments to others. The capacity to form reciprocal and intimate relationships develops, and the ability to compromise and be self-sacrificing emerges. The inability to form such relationships can lead to depression, isolation, and loneliness.

This is also the stage where having children is introduced into one's life. As a person is transitioning into this stage of development, one critical question becomes apparent: "Can I give fully of myself to others?" This internal question of submitting your identity to the needs and care of others gives rise to the virtue of love.

As a church, the most vital time for stability and growth occurs when a child of God enters this point of his spiritual life. He's looking to develop committed relationships with other members of the church. He's begun to establish his identity in Christ, and the purpose God has given him begins to manifest. He has initiative, a willingness to help others, and a desire to connect with others. The church is part of who this child of God is. The church is the active component of growth and health in the body of Christ.

As a church, we must embrace these individuals and help demonstrate what a committed relationship within the church looks like. We must watch for those who seem to be isolated and disconnected from the body. Reach for them and, as a church, be the ones to initiate intimate, spiritual relationships.

If we ourselves are at this stage in our spiritual maturity, we must begin to seek out intimate relationships within the church. The success of this stage relies upon our ability to "do life" or "live out our faith" with others. Having a group of accountability partners, confidants, prayer partners, mentors, and advisors will add depth to our spiritual maturity.

Developing relationships with those who are not as spiritually mature is also vitally important. You have received a great deal of nurturing from others, so now is the time to return the favor.

In this phase of our spiritual development, we are learning to love as Christ loved the church. It will require sacrifice and denying our own desires. The love of God will become a major part of our worldview, and the extent to which we embrace this love will determine the level of intimacy we have with God, people within our church family, and those in the community at large.

If we focus on the cares of life and the things of the world during this phase of our spiritual development, we'll find ourselves drifting away from the church and from God. At this critical phase, we must learn to crucify our flesh and its desires for the sake of God's calling on our lives.

Care

The seventh stage of psychosocial development laid out by Erikson is generativity versus stagnation. This stage is defined by the existential question, "Can I make my life count?"

This developmental stage of life is when people begin to live out their destinies. For many, this is the time when they're working in their career, raising their kids, giving back to society, and becoming a part of the bigger picture. This time can be rewarding for some but depressing for others.

The plans of youth may not have been fulfilled; jobs may be mundane. A dead-end life can lead to feelings of stagnation and lack of purpose. People can become self-centered.

At this time, the question arises, "What can I offer the next generation?" We should begin to focus on our influence on others' lives. We should become less concerned about what people think and more focused on how we can make this influence positive.

This stage of life can have two outcomes depending on a person's view of his status. If he feels he's transitioned successfully into adulthood and is productive, he'll mature into the primary task of this stage—care. By helping to guide future generations and contributing to society, this person will demonstrate the attributes that come from a life lived well. However, if he is unwilling to help, he'll become dissatisfied with his life and stagnate in his maturity, leading a life that lacks productivity.

As a church, we should be the embodiment of this stage. We should be demonstrating to others how to be caring. Throughout the various developmental stages, we as a church should play a vital role. If we've done our job up to this point, those who are entering into this stage will have experienced the virtue of true care. They'll have seen it manifest in the love and lives of the people in their community.

As a church, there's no greater reward than seeing those who have matured under our care reach a point where they're giving back to the next generation. It's been said the church is one generation away from extinction. If we fail to mature the next spiritual generation to the point of caring for others, the church will become nonexistent.

If we are at this stage in our spiritual maturity, we must evaluate the task that has been placed in our care. We are now in the role of our God-given destiny—we've become "the church," the representation of the Kingdom of Heaven on Earth. The world is depending on us to be the sons of God, to manifest God's character into this world. A great responsibility rests on our shoulders, and we must grow up and take on an active role in the church.

There's no one to do it for us. It's no one's responsibility but ours. If we don't take on the role of caring for the future generation, the church will stagnate. The church will not be productive. We'll become dissatisfied with our congregation and begin jumping from place to place, looking for purpose and motivation.

At this time in our lives, we must not neglect our duty as children of God. The health of His Kingdom is in our hands. The weight of a lost world has been placed in our care. We must grow up.

Wisdom

The eighth stage of psychosocial development laid out by Erikson is ego integrity versus despair. This stage is defined by the existential question, "Is it OK to have been me?"

As people get older, they begin to slow down. They don't explore the world as readily as they once did, and their productivity decreases. During this time in a person's life, he begins to evaluate his accomplishments and quantify the value of his life-long contributions. Those who feel they were unproductive or did not reach their goals become depressed and hopeless from the feelings of dissatisfaction and despair. A person who sees his life as happy, full of accomplishments, and productive will feel contentment and integrity in his life.

This stage can occur out of sequence if a person is faced with a terminal diagnosis. Many times, people are faced with life-altering news, news that they may not have long to live, or a near-death experience begin to evaluate their lives. They contemplate their legacy or impact. At these times, their focus shifts from their own personal ambitions and desires to passing on the wisdom they have learned through their life or acknowledging the futile way they have lived the life they were given.

As a church, our role is to identify people experiencing this stage in their lives and bring encouragement. As elder saints reach the point where they're not physically capable of doing what they once could, they begin to feel valueless. From the standpoint of Christ, our work is not complete until we pass from this life into eternity.

At this point, as a church, we must intentionally lay the foundation for these maturing children of God to re-address the prior developmental stage in their life: the generativity vs. stagnation stage. We must help them find a new purpose, so they can be productive. We must help them take the wisdom they have gained through a life well lived and impart it to the lives of others.

There is no room for retirement in the family of God. We'll find new roles to fill and new mountains to conquer. If we see someone in the prime of his or her Christian walk facing this stage of development, we must evaluate the underlying cause. What has transpired to bring about this level of despair?

At the core of this stage is the feeling that things are coming to an end. There are a number of things that can elicit a terminal mindset in the heart of a child of God. As a church, we must become spiritual cardiologists, find out what the underlying pathology is, and treat the disease, not just the symptoms.

If we're at this stage in our spiritual maturity, we may ask ourselves, "Have I found contentment through my life?" However, while we still breathe, we have work to do. We must begin to evaluate our purpose and the plan God has for us. We've gained a lot of wisdom over the years of walking with Christ. We have stories of His greatness that can encourage others passing through their own storms and trials.

We still have much to give to others. Write a book, tell your life's story, start a new ministry. All of these accomplishments are within our reach. We have, residing within us, wisdom and knowledge that can change the world. You can inspire and lead others to greatness. When we evaluate the end of our Christian walk, we need to stop and remind ourselves that "we are still here." If we're still here, He still has a purpose for us to fulfill. Let's apply the wisdom we've received through our lives and press on to perfection.

Chapter Seven

The Five-Fold Ministry – The Process of Maturation

"For when for the time ye ought to be teachers, ye have need that one teach you again which be the first principles of the oracles of God; and are become such as have need of milk, and not of strong meat. For every one that useth milk is unskilful in the word of righteousness: for he is a babe. But strong meat belongeth to them that are of full age, even those who by reason of use have their senses exercised to discern both good and evil."

(Hebrews 5:12-14 [KJV])

In the development of a child, there are milestones we measure to evaluate the progression of his maturity. Numerous tests and measurements are taken to rank the child according to his age, height, head circumference, etc. It's a fact that maturing is a process. There are points we can detect; there are visible markers of the development.

These measurable variables are directly linked to systems within the body that are set in motion at conception. As these systems develop, they display outward manifestations of their internal maturation.

For instance, the process of sexual maturity can be defined by distinct stages. These stages indicate what point along the continuum the child is currently at in his progression toward maturity.

This maturation of sexual reproduction, in both males and females, is a combination of various processes within the body working together to create visible changes in the child's growth. Each of these processes is required and serves a distinct function. The loss of any of these processes can result in children not reaching their full potential. It can affect their height, their bone development, and even their ability to produce children.

Within the context of the church, there is a similar culmination of processes that facilitate the progression of maturation. Paul talks about these systems in Ephesians:

> *"From whom the whole body fitly joined together and compacted by that which every joint supplieth, according to the effectual working in the measure of every part, maketh increase of the body unto the edifying of itself in love."*
>
> (Ephesians 4:16 [KJV])

As a child goes through the process of maturation, the father's contribution is vital for providing guidance and support, nurturing the child's character, and mentoring the child to fulfill his role as a part of the family.

God is into systems. He designed the universe to revolve in a circuit. The order of nature is a set of repetitive cycles that intricately function to manifest and maintain God's creative work.

The family is much the same. A mother and a father play vital roles within the structure of a family. They train their children to grow and replicate their roles in caring for future generations.

Just as our body matures, just as a family grows and nurtures its children, each part of the body and each member of the family have vital roles to play. God has placed within His church specific processes that are critical to the maturation of His children.

> *"And he gave some, apostles; and some, prophets; and some, evangelists; and some, pastors and teachers; For the perfecting of the saints, for the work of the ministry, for the edifying of the body of Christ: Till we all come in the unity of the faith, and of the knowledge of the Son of God, unto a perfect man, unto the measure of the stature of the fulness of Christ:"*
>
> (Ephesians 4:11-13 [KJV])

Many have read this scripture and know it by heart. It's been referred to as the five-fold ministry. God has placed these ministerial roles upon certain people. However, in the context of this passage, we see these ministerial roles culminate to a specific purpose: to nurture the body, so we attain adulthood. Many have lost sight of the proper function of these ministries. Some people see them as a hierarchical stratum of leadership, which defines their position and how they must use their power over others.

God didn't leave Himself out of the active role of nurturing His children. He takes on an intimate role in their development. He placed within the church the gifts of apostles, prophets, evangelists, pastors, and teachers to create an optimal environment for His presence to nurture His children.

These roles are the culmination of the attributes of a loving father working in conjunction with the mother to bring about a culture of optimal growth and development. Each role fulfills a process in the child's development. These processes provide an opportunity for God to manifest Himself and interact with His children in a fatherly role. As the mother, the church puts these roles in action and provides the foundation upon which the children of God can be directed into a stronger relationship with their Father.

The Apostle's Process

The first position God gave the church was that of the apostle, as described in 1 Corinthians 12:28. The Greek word for apostle is *apostolos*, which according to Strong's concordance, means "a messenger, envoy, delegate, or one commissioned by another to represent him in some way" (Strong 2010).

The word *apostolos* was originally a secular term. In ancient Greece and Rome, it referred to special envoys who were sent out to establish the dominion of the empire over a territory. These apostolos were commissioned to establish, train, instruct, convert, conquer, and subdue the new subjects of the territory and establish the culture of the empire within that new land. In practice, the apostolos was sent in the full authority and power of the emperor. The apostolos were the pioneers of new territory for the Greek and Roman Empires.

In Jewish culture, during the time of Christ, the word apostolos corresponded to an Old Testament word, "Sheliach or shaliach," which means "agent or emissary." This word is a halachic (Torah-legal) term, describing a person given the authority to act in the place of someone else. This means the person receiving the commission is exactly like the person who commissioned him.

With this understanding, we can see the function of apostles is to act in the authority of who sent them. The proper functioning of this gift will change the environment in which the apostle is operating.

As we're growing and maturing in Christ, we'll thrive best when we're in the proper environment for our growth potential and development. The Lord has placed within His church people and groups who can and will manifest the environment essential for our optimal growth. These people will act as an example of Christ in our lives.

These people create an atmosphere that reflects the King, our Father. Much like a mother sets the tone and atmosphere of the home, the church atmosphere is established by the "*apostolos.*" They're the manifestation of the government of the empire of Christ. Their presence alters our lives. They manifest the miraculous gifts of the Kingdom and subdue all of the opposing spiritual influences in our environment.

These people are essential to our development. The apostle's process creates an environment where God is directly manifest in our lives. These people are able to create an environment for the Holy Spirit to explore the new territories within our hearts that we've kept hidden or tried to avoid. They help empower us to explore these territories. Walking alongside us, they act as our guide so we can manifest the Kingdom culture throughout every aspect of our life.

This process will result in the establishment of the culture of the Kingdom of Heaven. It will convert those who are living contrary to the laws of the Kingdom. It'll conquer the areas of resistance that have taken up strongholds in our lives. It'll subdue the works of the flesh.

When this process begins, we must face ourselves—our true selves. The manifestation of the Kingdom will shine the light of truth into all the recesses of our hearts. The remnants of the old culture of sin will change when we allow ourselves to be subject to the process of the apostle's gift.

The Prophet's Process

The prophet is the next process listed in Ephesians. The Greek word *prophétés*, which according to Strong's concordance, means "a prophet, poet;

a person gifted at expositing divine truth." More accurately, it implies someone who "declares the mind (message) of God, which sometimes predicts the future (foretelling) and, more commonly, speaks forth His message for a particular situation" (Strong 2010).

The position of the prophet goes back to the beginning of the Biblical story. An extra-biblical narrative indicates that Adam himself was a prophet who foretold things that were to come. The list of the men who God used to speak forth His message, including both Enoch and Noah, is extensive.

For every prophet that God used, He had a purpose. He was fulfilling a process. God ordained events to be manifest at *kairos* moments, and He uses prophets to communicate with us. He selected men to speak His will, His future, His plan, His mind, and His message to those around them. The creative power of God's breath exists within every one of us, and God will use the voice of a man to speak His will into existence.

At various times in the Old Testament, God used prophets in a wide range of settings. God's overall purpose in using the prophets was to manifest His will into the lives of men. Within the church, this purpose remains intact. God desires to see His will manifest in our lives.

The process of a prophet is to speak life into the intention of God's purpose in particular situations. This process utilizes the creative power of the breath of God within us to speak into existence things of the spiritual realm into the natural realm.

We all instinctively long for someone to speak about our future or to compliment us on something we've done. Along with the compliment, we desire someone to tell us how our current efforts are going to manifest greatness in our lives. Each of us instinctively knows the power of the spoken word. However, we often fail to utilize this power by speaking into the lives of others.

The process of the prophet takes this reality to a different level. In the case of a prophet, it's not a person speaking positively about our future. It's not a man telling of things that are to come to pass. In the case of a prophet, it's God speaking into our lives. It's our heavenly Father telling us we're going to be great or warning us to be prepared for what's to come. It's God's voice directing what we're intended to be and calling out within us our destiny along with the results of our disobedience. It's God telling us about the *kairos* moments He has prepared before us. It's God acknowledging our skills, traits, and talents.

For our true spiritual selves to mature, we require this input from our Heavenly Father. Children need a father who tells them how great they're going to be. It sets the stage for greatness to manifest in their lives. The children of God are no different. For this reason, God created the prophet's process.

There are attributes of God within us that lay dormant. These attributes, talents, and spiritual traits sometimes need to be called out before we can focus our attention on nurturing them to maturity. A good example of this is a child who has an amazing singing voice. To the child, it may just be fun to sing. When someone notices this talent and speaks encouragement into the child, this talent becomes an area in which the child places effort. It becomes an area of confidence for the child.

Sometimes, all a prophet is doing is calling out those spiritual traits we received through regeneration. Other times, a prophet may be calling to life those traits that were once alive within us, but through spiritual neglect, we had allowed to die. At other times, a prophet may identify aspects of our lives that aren't true to our new nature or a remnant of our old selves.

Moreover, a prophet may forewarn us, so we can be prepared for what is to come. In these instances, we must remember God doesn't forewarn us to scare us. He forewarns us to prepare us. Whatever the nature of the prophecy, the process produces the same result, to call forth the will and destiny of God.

We must also understand the prophetic words are eternal in nature. We must take these words and pray them into our natural reality. In the case of prophetic words of warning, we must pray to prevent the outcome, for a way to escape, or to strengthen our spirit to endure what is to come. Seeking God for wisdom and guidance will help clarify how we are to pray. Many times, I have failed to understand the prophetic in my own life. God has told me of things to come, and I did not seek His guidance. Many of these times, if I had prayed, I could have avoided many problems in my life.

Jonah delivered a prophetic word to Nineveh in the Old Testament. The citizens of Nineveh responded by praying to God and repenting. This act changed the outcome of the prophetic word from destruction to salvation.

The prophetic process plays a role in the chastisement of God toward his children. God sent His word and gave us the scripture to provide guidance for us. In 2 Timothy, the Lord outlines the function of the scripture.

> *"All scripture is given by inspiration of God, and is profitable for doctrine, for reproof, for correction, for instruction in righteousness: That the man of God may be perfect, throughly furnished unto all good works."*
>
> (2 Timothy 3:16-17 [KJV])

The spoken Word of God is powerful, even more, powerful than a double-edged sword. However, the function of the Word is to edify the church. Nevertheless, there are times when disobedience must be dealt with, and sin must be addressed. This is the function of the Word presented through the process of the prophet. There is a distinction between the prophet and the pastor. Many times, a modern-day pastor wears both hats, if not all the hats of these processes.

The declaration of the inspired Word will bring a person to a point where he realizes he's doing wrong. It'll enlighten him and teach him how to correct his shortcoming. Edicts, mandates, memos, memorandums, and church standards can never bring about an internal change in the soul. Only the Word of God can affect that kind of change. The process God set in place to manifest the life-changing power of His word is prophetic.

The amazing thing about the process of a prophet is the ability to prophesy to oneself. Everyone has heard of a self-fulfilling prophecy. I'm sure each of us experienced it at least once in our own lives. We speak of something, and it comes to pass. Sometimes we forget our words are carried on the creative breath of God. Our idle words can manifest a negative outcome with debilitating consequences.

We must learn to speak over ourselves, calling out those things that are within us. We must speak the manifestation of the characteristics of God into existence in our lives. We must bring to life the righteousness of God within us and within our families and loved ones. We must prophesy blessings over our kids. I believe this is one of the reasons Paul desired all would prophesy.

> *"I would that ye all spake with tongues, but rather that ye prophesied: for greater is he that prophesieth than he that speaketh with tongues, except he interpret, that the church may receive edifying."*
>
> (1 Corinthians 14:5 [KJV])

The prophetic process is vital, and we all can play a role. There are those who prophesy at levels many of us do not understand because God uses people at different levels to perform the process. We all have experienced prophesy in operation in our lives. Some may recognize those events distinctly, and others may have experienced prophetic events without noticing them. Nevertheless, it's required for all of us to reach our full potential in Christ.

There's nothing more precious to children than to have their father take notice of something they have done and offer encouragement. Nothing gives children more motivation than their father telling them what wonderful gifts they have or what great potential they have. This is one of the greatest functions of the prophet: edifying the children of God.

The Evangelist's Process

The next process in God's maturation system is the evangelist. The Greek word *euaggelistés* means "an evangelist, bearer of good tidings," according to Strong's concordance (Strong 2010). In the Greco-Roman culture, the word had the connotation of someone who delivered or heralded important news or events for the empire.

In Christianity, this concept has taken on various connotations. An orator who comes to a church and preaches a message to revive the congregation is known as an evangelist. Although this position is more like that of a revivalist, it still holds some of the original evangelist purpose. By speaking of the events of the Kingdom, the greatness of God, and the news of God moving in the various communities within the body, the modern-day evangelist fulfills part of their original function.

To fully understand the role of the evangelist in the Greco-Roman empires, we must look at the culture itself. The means of communication in the time of Christ were limited. No one could just Google the email address for the Roman Gazette and send a story of a local marriage taking place in Bethlehem of Judea. There was no Facebook or internet-based Hieroglyphic scroll. They couldn't send out a multi-recipient text message to their entire circle of loved ones inviting them to the bridal shower. Someone had to deliver messages personally.

This was a very difficult task, and it required a great deal of travel. In most cases, the message had to be delivered verbally. If the message was intended for multiple recipients in multiple locations, the process could take months.

Positive announcements were always a welcome event. The government used the evangelist to spread good news within the empire. What a great way to build the morale of the Kingdom! It also offset any negative publicity that may have been circulating by word of mouth.

Within the context of the church, this took on an amazing role. The evangelist would go into areas and deliver the message of the good news of the gospel to those who had not heard it. They would convey the events of an outpouring of God in the churches in Asia Minor and deliver it to other churches. Various other events were conveyed in a similar fashion. An evangelist would have heralded the news of Paul or other ministers coming to an area.

All of this resulted in God communicating to His family, the body of Christ, that new children were being born. It communicated the great works that His children were doing in their various locations. It was God's way of bragging to everyone about the efforts of His children.

There are two things that children will sit and listen to. One is the voice of their father telling other people how proud he is of them and the back-story of what lead up to the events that made him so proud. The second is listening to their dad tell a story about himself. Children love stories.

The process of the evangelist allows God to brag about His kids and tell His kids about Himself. The evangelist is a storyteller. He tells the story of redemption by preaching the Gospel, the good news. He tells the story of who brought such a great change to our lives. He tells the story of God working presently in the lives of His children. He tells the stories of how God's children are growing in grace and truth.

The evangelist tells us about the history of our family. These stories allow us to know our family, to know how our family came to be, to know how it works together. We can see more clearly our role and the part we play.

The Pastor's Process

The next process in God's maturing system is the pastor. The Greek word *poimén* means "a shepherd; the feeder, protector, and ruler of a flock," according to Strong's concordance (Strong 2010).

The task of caring for a flock of sheep is not as easy as it sounds. During the time of Christ, shepherds were very busy people. They had to lead their flocks to pastures to graze. They had to take them to places to drink. If this water came from a well, the pastor would have to use something to get the water for the flock. They had to keep their eyes out for predators. They had to keep an eye on the sheep at all times.

There was no window for taking a vacation. They were shepherds, and their sheep were their life and livelihood. They spent countless hours in the fields, fought off bears and lions, tended to the sheep's medical needs, and sheered them at least once or twice a year. Being a shepherd was a full-time job.

Anyone who's ever been around sheep knows they're an interesting animal to work with. They're not like cattle or horses. You can domesticate a horse and ride it; a horse develops a specific bond with its rider. The rider learns the nature of the horse, and the horse learns the nature of the rider. A horse and rider can drive cattle. You can drive a herd of cattle toward a given destination.

Sheep are a different breed of animal. If you attempt to drive sheep, they scatter. They are easy to spook given the proper stimulus. To move sheep into a given direction, you either need a sheepdog that is trained to wrangle the sheep, or you need to train the sheep to follow the shepherd.

Sheep who know the voice of the shepherd are easy to gather together. They are not easily scattered. Nevertheless, sheep must be led. The shepherd has to blaze the trail. The shepherd has to ensure the environment is clear of dangers that may scatter them or cause harm.

The shepherd's rod and staff were meant to pull the sheep back toward the flock or to fight off a predator's attack. The rod and the staff were never meant to be raised in punishment.

The process of the pastor is not to beat the sheep into submission but to lead the sheep to nourishment and guide them to fulfill their purpose.

Every person on the face of the earth is a child of God. Some have experienced the new birth and the new nature that accompanies regeneration; some are unborn children waiting for conception and birth to take place. All are descended from Adam and Eve; all are of the pedigree of the Garden of Eden. Therefore, every man, woman, boy, and girl fall under the second job given to man by God, "to cultivate and protect the things of the garden." A pastor's role is not to subjugate the flock but to be a loving mentor and coach, to be an example, and encourage children of God toward their purpose.

Holiness and righteousness can't be mandated. The Old Testament law demonstrated the fallacy in this approach. The only way a person can truly be holy and righteous is through the working of the Holy Ghost within his life. True holiness manifests when the child of God recognizes he is destined for a unique purpose in the Kingdom of God. He must come to this revelation and fully believe this fact in his spirit. This acknowledgment of being set apart for a divine purpose is the epitome of holiness. Once this revelation has been achieved, the next task is to guide the child of God to make appropriate choices that lead to his God-given destiny.

By directing the decisions of the children of God, we bring them to a point where they can focus on manifesting the character required for fulfilling their purpose. This process is true righteousness.

The pastor's process involves leading God's children to the understanding of their purpose in the Kingdom and encouraging them to press toward its manifestation. The pastor must lead the child to the right nourishment required for growth and direct the child to the proper grazing area required for nourishment.

These statements may sound odd concerning the view of a pastor's role in today's church world. Many great pastors are out there, pastoring multiple churches. Many of these pastors know they have people within their congregation who are called to great heights, but as pastors, they feel ineffective in their ability to coach those people toward the fulfillment of their destiny. They see this as a sign of weakness or insecurity. God places people in areas for a season, then moves them for their development's sake. Some need a little extra prodding to help them take the proper steps toward their destiny.

A child starts in a bassinet and moves to a crib. Before too long, they are in a regular bed. If a child failed to grow to the next level and remained in the baby bed for the duration of his life, there would be a problem.

Every mother has experienced that moment in her child's life where he or she transitions from baby to toddler—especially if it's the last child, and the mother knows this will be her last baby. The pain of the child's maturation becomes a point of heartache for the mother. Nevertheless, the child must grow, even at her despair.

This is even true in the family of God. People may be under the care of a given pastor for a season before he moves to a new location. Alternatively, God may ask the pastor to approach a member of the church with an opportunity to go and work at a different location, or He may ask a new pastor to help children of God mature in ways that may not be possible in the current setting. When these times come, they can be painful to the church family and the pastor. They may even be hard for the pastor to understand.

The pastor's process is one of maturing children to a point where they can become independent in the manifestation of their destiny. Just as a mother nurtures and coaches her children to become independent, pastors provide the same support for children of God.

It may mean the parent drops the child off to a coach who specializes in football, baseball, running, or playing a musical instrument. In the end, the growth and development of the child are the most critical aspect of parenting. The same is true in the pastor's process.

An amazing thing about the process of the pastor is that it primarily doesn't occur in the pulpit. The true process of the pastor takes place by living life with the children whom God has placed under his care. Standing up on a platform and delivering a sermon can provide great motivation for the team as a whole. However, to influence the sheep, you must live with the sheep.

If an old-world shepherd stepped out in the middle of the sheep enclosure and gave a charismatic message to the sheep—telling them how great they were going to do today eating the grass and drinking the water before going back into the house and waiting for the sheep to take care of themselves—I am confident the sheep wouldn't feel they were being taken care of, nor would they thrive.

The same is true of a pastor. The pastor's influence is not seen in the inspiring sermon but in a life lived touching the flock daily—leading and guiding them, caring for their hurts and needs, ensuring they receive proper nourishment, speaking an encouraging word into their life at the appropriate moment. This is the ministry of a pastor.

The process of a pastor is a loving mother helping a child by interacting with them daily, sitting down at imaginary tea parties or tossing the ball in the yard, all the while listening to the child, acknowledging the child's unique attributes, and speaking life into their destiny, calling them to stretch themselves to their full potential. God places pastors into our lives to be our role models and a source of inspiration.

The Teacher's Process

The next process in God's maturing system is the teacher. The Greek word *didaskalos* means "a teacher, an instructor acknowledged for their mastery in their field of learning," according to Strong's concordance (Strong 2010).

To understand the nature of a teacher, we must put the role in the context of the time of Christ. Much like modern-day apprenticeships, trades were passed from father to son or child to artisan through the art of hands-on work experience. The master craftsman would take a young apprentice into his care and agree to train the child in his trade. Historically, the young apprentice was legally bound to the craftsman. He was the expert in the field of study and took on the role of the teacher.

In the context of the scripture, this relationship involves a teacher and a disciple. It's amazing to note that Jesus didn't come as an apostle, a prophet, an evangelist, or a pastor—Jesus came as a teacher.

> *"The same came to Jesus by night, and said unto him, Rabbi, we know that thou art a teacher come from God: for no man can do these miracles that thou doest, except God be with him."*
>
> (John 3:2 [KJV]).

Jesus didn't take on the role of the good shepherd, or pastor, until the time of his crucifixion. He even attests to the fact that the defining factor of His role as a pastor would be exemplified by His death.

> *"I am the good shepherd. The good shepherd gives His life for the sheep."*
>
> (John 10:11 [KJV]).

His ministry illustrates the role He filled as a teacher. His disciples were trained by His teaching. His acts and miracles were performed to provide examples for us.

In the homes of tradesmen who had sons, the job of master craftsman or teacher was taken on by the father. From the time the son was able to perform the smallest task associated with his future trade, he could be found with his father working at the family business. This father-son apprenticeship was the primary source of education for hundreds of years. The apprenticeship was a coveted position in many career paths.

Today, much of this culture has been lost, and this type of relationship between children and their fathers has been lost. At the time of Christ, this was still a very relevant model of education.

Within the context of the church, the role of teacher today doesn't hold the connotation that it held during the time of the early church. Many times, we only view teachers as those individuals who take care of the children in Sunday school. In reality, the process of the teacher reaches deep into the lives of the children of God.

Because this role has, in many instances, lost its relevance to our society, we fail to properly establish this process within the modern church. The maturation process of an individual requires that proper training take place for a child to enter into the role and position he's designed to fill. Failure to train a child properly to fulfill their role will result in frustration and feelings of inadequacy and hopelessness.

The process of the teacher plays a vital role in bringing about the transition from a child to a mature son or daughter of God. The fulfillment of our destiny is predicated upon being properly equipped to accomplish the task associated with our purpose.

A loving father knows how to properly equip and train a child to maximize their potential and optimize their skill set. God placed teachers in the church to maximize His children's effectiveness in the Kingdom. Every step of the development of a child requires training and the development of knowledge and skills. Many educational models exist to optimize curriculum performance for students in professional programs.

In the case of the church, it behooves us to take a second look at our educational process for the maturation of God's children.

God placed the role of the teacher within the body of the church to serve as instructors to help bring up, educate, train, and equip children for the work of the Kingdom. The absence of this process results in underdeveloped children with a lack of purpose, sense of responsibility, and ownership. The process of the teacher is one of the most critical processes in the Kingdom. This process continues throughout the life of a mature child of God.

The Combined Process

All of these processes are the direct manifestation of the character of God. God knows the family needs a father and a mother. He also knows a child truly can't mature into the full stature of his genetic makeup without the nurturing of a father and mother.

For this reason, God placed these roles and positions within the church. They aren't positions to be obtained or fought over. One is not greater than the other. There aren't the apostles at the top of the heap and the teachers at the bottom. There is a divine order to these processes in a child of God's life.

Parents working together set the environment of the household. Parents fill the role of speaking into the child's life, his destiny, and design. They tell their child the family's purpose and how he fits into the family. Parents tell everyone about the child's accomplishments. The parents tell the stories of the family's history. Parents coach and mentor their children through various phases of his life. Parents teach their children the family business and take them under their wing as young apprentices.

In the same way, a father working with the mother cares for his child, our Heavenly Father has placed these vital positions in the church, so He can operate through these offices to bring His children to their full potential.

> *"For the perfecting of the saints, for the work of the ministry, for the edifying of the body of Christ: Till we all come in the unity of the faith, and of the knowledge of the Son of God, unto a perfect man, unto the measure of the stature of the fulness of Christ:"*
>
> (Ephesians 4:12-13 [KJV])

The combination of these processes is to bring about one goal. For every child of God to become like Christ, the church must have trained people to perform the work of the ministry. This doesn't happen accidentally. God implemented a strategy to train and equip people to work in the Kingdom. That process is outlined in these ministerial roles.

The process begins with the apostle. Before we can mature into the full stature of Christ, we must have the proper environment. Then we must see ourselves for who we are and who God has made us to be. We need someone to encourage us and mentor us to grow in grace. Finally, we have to make ourselves teachable.

Many people see the roles outlined in this process as a hierarchical structure. They try to work their way to the top. They call themselves apostles and demand subjugation. This pursuit of position is not the pattern God designed. The Kingdom is not about the pursuit of position but the pursuit of purpose. To pursue our purpose, we must submit ourselves wholly to be taught by the Holy Spirit.

When we become teachable, our destiny becomes reachable. Our destiny and purpose in this new life are not to fill a position; it's to change the environment. You don't need a title to change your world. You don't need the approval of men to give your ministry influence. Most of our growth in Christ occurs when He is taking us into the realm of our inabilities. The only way we can become what God has destined us to be is to come to the realization that it's not by our might nor by our power but by the Spirit of the Lord that we will fulfill our spiritual destiny.

Too many times, we fall upon our own talent and skill or have our own plans and methods. These aren't bad to have. Joseph developed a number of skills and talents as a slave in Potiphar's house and as the keeper of the prison. Nevertheless, none of Joseph's skills were able to bring him out of prison and before the presence of the pharaoh. God used other people to bring Joseph to power. Additionally, God used the supernatural gift of dream interpretation to establish Joseph's authority—a gift that only came from God.

Joseph, in his own power, couldn't have interpreted the dream of the pharaoh. Joseph, in his own power, couldn't have commanded an audience with the pharaoh. To solidify Joseph's destiny, God used His Spirit operating through mechanisms outside of the control of Joseph, so in the end, Joseph had no room to boast that he had brought about his destiny by his own might.

God will use your time of growth to train you for your destiny with His own spiritual methods, so in the end, you will have no other option but to glorify Him for bringing about your success.

God placed these various processes within the church to bring about your education for spiritual maturity. You'll grow at your own level of obedience to God's educational processes. For spiritual growth, you must become like a little child in the care of his Father. You must submit yourself to the environment of the family. You must listen to the destiny God has prepared for you. You listen as God rejoices over your successes. Let Him coach you. You must become teachable in the hands of the master. The only way to reach your full potential is to see yourself as the child of God that you are and throw yourself in His arms.

My wife's father died when she was 16. We have been married for more than 18 years, and she still misses him. There is nothing that can replace a father or a mother in your life. Once they have gone, you realize how much they impacted your life. The function of a father in a family is different from the role of the mother. The role of the mother in a family is different from that of a father. In most instances, the father in a family is not good at trying to be the mother. There's just something about a mom that a dad can't replace, just as there are things about a dad that a mom can't replace.

When a parent is lost, all of the aspects of raising a child are placed on one parent, the functional unit of the family is impacted. When the mother takes on all the responsibility of the family, the mother may feel overwhelmed. The same is true with the father; when the touch of a mother is lost, things become different. Many studies have shown the impact of single-parent families on children, indicating that they are likely to do poorly in some measures compared to children of a married couple (Jeffreys 2019).

The same is true in the Kingdom of God. God has placed within his Kingdom a church, which serves the role of the mother and the process of the fivefold ministry to direct His children to a more intimate relationship with the Father. If all the responsibility is placed upon one of these two units and not shared equally, then the family begins to suffer.

The job of the church and the working of the five-fold-maturing process is not to point the child of God to a set of doctrinal dogmas, ordinances, or standardized creeds. The role of the church and the ministry is to point the child to a relationship with God.

In many churches, all the work of the church and the ministry is placed upon the shoulders of the pastor. He must be the apostle, the prophet, the evangelist, the teacher, and the mother to all the children in the church. This can be seen in the statistical analysis of pastors.

In 2018, the average length of a pastor's tenure was only 6 years (Blackwell 2018). There are a number of variables that play into this statistic, but the brevity of the tenure speaks volumes to the role the pastor is expected to play in the church.

The Kingdom of God is the manifestation of His family. All the elements of the family unit are present and accounted for. All of these elements have a unique and critical role to play. Understanding these roles and how they function together within the system of the church is vital to its stability and health.

Many church members have no idea what their role in the family of God is. Many pastors are struggling to fill all the roles. This role confusion is a result of the church changing to resemble the world or the world imitating the church.

It's vital we begin to understand the functioning of these processes within the family of God and the unique roles each of us plays. The combination of all of these processes creates the environment and the structure God put in place to raise His children to their full potential.

We're all critical to the proper functioning of the Kingdom and the family of God. We must become students of God's design. When we all come together in the unity of the faith with one mind and one purpose, taking our rightful position in the full manifestation of the Kingdom, limitless power will manifest.

Chapter Eight

Growing in Righteousness – Onus of Righteousness

"But unto you that fear my name shall the Sun of righteousness arise with healing in his wings; and ye shall go forth, and grow up as calves of the stall."
(Malachi 4:2 [KJV]).

Righteousness is concomitant with right standing with God and being equitable with His character. Through regeneration, we've been made God's righteousness. We've been spiritually transformed into his likeness, possessing the characteristics and traits of God our Father.

Genetics is an amazing mechanism created by God to pass along parental traits to offspring. This coded message can produce the most amazing characteristics and abilities in our progeny. There remains but one factor that can inhibit the manifestation of these traits: if the parental roles are filled, if negative environmental factors are eliminated, if the proper food, nutrients, and energy are supplied, but the child doesn't exert effort to master his natural-born abilities, these traits won't manifest.

A child with the capacity to be the next Olympic gold medalist won't be successful if he never takes ownership of his potential and takes training seriously, even if all the genetics are present and if every other factor is optimally aligned.

There is an onus to one's genetic potential. The full weight of the responsibility of becoming who we were born to become rests in our hands. The choices we make affect the degree to which we live up to our potential. The only way to become all that we can be is to take an active role in nurturing and cultivating the abilities we were born with. The onus is on us.

Potential has no ability to make an external impact unless the potential is released to become kinetic. The same is true with our spiritual nature and the righteousness that's been placed within us. We have the potential to manifest every characteristic and trait associated with God if we take on the responsibility.

> *"And it shall be our righteousness, if we observe to do all these commandments before the LORD our God, as he hath commanded us."*
>
> (Deuteronomy 6:25 [KJV])

Lack of motivation can become a problem when training. Athletes who desire to maximize their potential set grueling schedules for themselves. Limited personal freedom is a price to pay if athletes desire to be successful at what they do. There are things they don't eat. There are things they don't do. There are places they don't go. They evaluate their actions and choices through the lens of their destiny. If they wish to be the best, then they must forsake the rest. Anything that doesn't line up with their goal is forfeited for the prize that's set before them. An athlete will endure the pain of training to obtain their reward.

As possessors of God's characteristics, what are we willing to do to ensure His traits manifest in our lives? Are we willing to forgo comfort? Are we willing to give up perceived freedom? Are we willing to spend the time and effort required to see His nature shine within us?

The only way that'll ever happen is if we take on the responsibility. We know with assurance that if we step out and apply the required effort, make the needed sacrifices, and pay the price, we'll obtain what we seek. Not only will we find success, but we'll also find the happiness and blessings promised to those who manifest the righteousness of God.

> *"Blessed are they which do hunger and thirst after righteousness: for they shall be filled."*
>
> (Matthew 5:6 [KJV]).

Many athletes look back on the effort they exerted to reach their goals with regret. They neglected their family and, in some cases, their health. NFL football players serve as an example. Some have used performance-enhancing drugs and are now faced with the physiological and psychological consequences associated with that choice. Others have suffered traumatic head injuries from numerous concussions.

However, we have hope. We know the efforts we apply toward the pursuit of Godly righteousness will reap great rewards throughout our lives. We must take responsibility for the tasks and relationships God has placed in our care. The pursuit of true righteousness doesn't require the neglect of our God-given responsibilities to those placed in our care. Once we've obtained the full manifestation of Godly righteousness, we'll never look back on our lives and feel reproach for the effort and time we dedicated in its quest.

> *"My righteousness I hold fast, and will not let it go: my heart shall not reproach me so long as I live."*
>
> (Job 27:6 [KJV])

Righteousness isn't a destination you reach; it's a way of life. Much like living and eating healthily, a man's righteousness is not defined by a single moment but by a lifetime of the application of righteousness. It has to become a passion and driving motivation in our lives.

There will be times of struggle. There will be times when you feel you're the only one pursuing righteousness. Evil will surround you. It may seem like those who live ungodly lives prosper, and life will feel unfair. Nevertheless, we weren't called to live a life that's fair. We were called to live a life of grace—a life in God's favor where we receive what we don't deserve. It's a life of mercy where we aren't given the punishment we deserve. We must live a life that shows this same grace and mercy to others.

This is not a bad thing. In the end, the wicked will get their punishment, but if we live with righteousness, God will give us joy for our mourning. We will be exalted on this earth.

> *"Thou lovest righteousness, and hatest wickedness: therefore God, thy God, hath anointed thee with the oil of gladness above thy fellows."*
> (Psalm 45:7 [KJV]).

We must remember that we don't seek righteousness for the reward. We don't take on its responsibility because someone told us to. We take on the onus for righteousness because it's a part of our character, which is directly tied to our destiny. We must be righteous because we're born to be righteous.

Servants of Righteousness

We must remember we were once without hope. There was within us a nature that was contrary to the new nature we've received through regeneration. Our spiritual selves came alive with the transfer of God's genetic nature. Nevertheless, the memories and habits that once ruled our lives must be managed.

Because we have the power of life within our voice and can speak into existence things that are dead, we can resurrect the old nature that once ruled our lives. We can feed it by giving in to its desires. We can let it rule our thoughts and enslave us again.

The man we once were is dead, and our new life gives us the power to live free of the taskmaster of sin. However, if we choose to allow sin to rule our lives as it once ruled our fallen nature, we subject our living soul, our new nature, to the bondage of sin and death.

We must determine within ourselves that we'll follow righteousness as if it is our new taskmaster. We must obey righteousness in all we do. We must not yield to our old nature; we must yield to the new nature.

> *"Know ye not, that to whom ye yield yourselves servants to obey, his servants ye are to whom ye obey; whether of sin unto death, or of obedience unto righteousness."*
>
> (Romans 6:16 [KJV])

How do we accomplish this task? How can we become a servant to righteousness? The task falls to us. We are the active component in this process. Righteousness will not enslave us; we must become its servant.

> *"Being then made free from sin, ye became the servants of righteousness. I speak after the manner of men because of the infirmity of your flesh: for as ye have yielded your members servants to uncleanness and to iniquity unto iniquity; even so now yield your members servants to righteousness unto holiness."*
>
> (Romans 6:18-19 [KJV])

We once gave no thought to our actions. We willingly allowed the desire of our flesh, the lust of our eye, and the pride of life to drive us to action. There appeared to be no choice in the matter. We did what felt right to ourselves. When we made our flesh happy, we were happy.

Just as we, without thought or resistance, followed after what the flesh wanted, we must yield ourselves completely to follow righteousness. If we resist it, the only alternative is sin. If we can't yield ourselves to righteousness, we're outside of God's will for our lives. It has to become our master, our teacher, our instructor, and our guide.

Our regenerated spiritual selves are created in righteousness and true holiness, just as Adam and Eve were created in the image of God and separated unto the purpose of God.

> *"And that ye put on the new man, which after God is created in righteousness and true holiness."*
>
> (Ephesians 4:24 [KJV]).

We must take ownership of the new person we've been transformed into. We can't allow the old nature of sin to rule our lives any longer. It's up to us to put away the habits of our old nature and to rein in every idle word, thought, or deed that doesn't match our new destiny. God has set before us the opportunity to live out a life of spiritual abundance, and it's up to us to decide who we serve.

Born of Righteousness

Our new birth gives us no option but to exist with the potential to be righteous. We have been born of righteousness.

"If ye know that He is righteous, ye know that every one that doeth righteousness is born of Him."

(1 John 2:29 [KJV])

The motivation to be righteous is not optional. The preference of our spiritual nature is to be righteous. If we allow our spiritual nature and the Spirit of God that resides within us to lead us and guide us into all truth, we'll do that which is right in God's eyes. We'll manifest His character.

"Little children, let no man deceive you: he that doeth righteousness is righteous, even as He is righteous."

(1 John 3:7 [KJV])

A problem arises when we quench the spiritual motivation within us and let the flesh take over. Our spiritual selves must be nurtured to grow. If we're to express the full array of our spiritual characteristics, we must ensure we position ourselves in the right conditions to achieve this outcome. No one else can do this for us. We can have the greatest mom in the world, our father can be the greatest dad the world has ever known, and we can have all the best teachers, but if we don't step up and accept who we were born to be, we'll never become what God intends.

If we allow things contrary to our new spiritual nature to govern our motivation and actions, we run the risk of reviving our old nature to which we were once enslaved. When we begin to cater to the desires of the flesh, we become the children of the devil. The devil gave Adam and Eve the desire to disobey God, to suffer a spiritual death, which resulted in a distorted, sinful nature. The devil, through deception, imparted to man the characteristics of sin, which gratified man's fleshly desires. To serve the flesh and nourish its desires is to acknowledge the parental contribution of the devil.

> *"In this the children of God are manifest, and the children of the devil: whosoever doeth not righteousness is not of God, neither he that loveth not his brother."*
>
> (1 John 3:10 [KJV])

Through Christ, we've received a new nature. We're no longer without hope driven about by the desires of the flesh. We now possess the power of the Holy Ghost to live above our carnal desires. We have a new motivation. Within us now resides the Spirit of God.

We have the Spirit of the living God within us, leading us and guiding us. We must not take the risk of quenching God's lead. The Spirit of God will direct us into areas of our life that need to grow. It may be uncomfortable. It may require that we extend ourselves. It may even require that we cast off things that are not agreeable to our destiny.

If we fail to allow the Spirit to lead us and guide us if we don't heed its lead if we quench the movement of God in our lives, we'll see that area of our lives fail to flourish, and that part of our spiritual nature die.

Much like the flow of blood through the veins of our body, the flow of the Spirit in our soul is required to bring nutrients, health, and resources to our life. These are required for growth. If we cut off the flow of blood to a portion of our body, that part of our body will die. The same is true if we quench the Spirit of God in our lives.

If we need to show others forgiveness in our lives, the Spirit of God will begin to flow in the area that leads us to seek out those we've failed to forgive. If there are areas that we need to avoid because they tempt us, the Spirit will begin to convict us. If we ignore the Spirit and quench its prodding, we'll become spiritually stunted. We may even run the risk of developing an area that becomes toxic to our whole spiritual nature.

We were born for righteousness. We were born to show the nature of Christ. We must allow the Spirit to flow through us and guide us into areas that need development.

Flee Unrighteousness

Many things in this life bid for our attention. So many things look good to our flesh and carnal desire. Advertisers know if they learn the mechanism behind what motivates people, they can use it to increase sales.

There are aspects of our human nature we must strive to understand. Things that motivate us to respond and react to our environment. These things, if left unchecked, can begin to rule our lives, even in the presence of religious habits.

Righteousness can become what we do instead of who we are. Righteous behaviors can become habits, and habits can become a religious ritual. In the end, we may not act righteously because we're righteous; we may just be following a pattern of behavior. When righteousness becomes a religious habit and not an act of our conscious effort, the flesh is not kept in check, and lust can begin to take root in our hearts. Once it is conceived, it can lead to sin if it's not crucified.

> *"But every man is tempted, when he is drawn away of his own lust, and enticed. Then when lust hath conceived, it bringeth forth sin: and sin, when it is finished, bringeth forth death."*
>
> (James 1:14-15 [KJV]).

We are born to a life led by the desires of the flesh. For many of us, this old sinful nature was a major part of our history. We have a strong memory of how we once lived, so much so that the memory can elicit pleasure, even after we've turned our lives over to Christ.

It's not an instantaneous fix when we're regenerated. We must make a conscious effort to eradicate the remnants of our old nature from our lives. We must remember our new nature is in its infancy when we first receive Christ into our lives. God gives us grace and mercy to grow up into righteousness. However, just because our spiritual selves have come alive and the old heart of sin has been remade, we must not forget our new nature is housed in a body that hasn't been glorified.

Because we're still housed in this body of death, as Apostle Paul referred to it in Romans 7:24, we must be vigilant to what drives our fleshly desires. Knowing our old nature will help us combat future sins. We must crucify the flesh with its passions and desires, as described in Galatians 5:24.

> *"And they that are Christ's have crucified the flesh with the affections and lusts."*
>
> (Galatians 5:24 [KJV])

> *"But thou, O man of God, flee these things; and follow after righteousness, godliness, faith, love, patience, meekness. Fight the good fight of faith, lay hold on eternal life, whereunto thou art also called, and hast professed a good profession before many witnesses."*
>
> (1 Timothy 6:11-12 [KJV])

We must intentionally seek out righteousness, godliness, faith, love, and patience and fight the good fight of faith, laying hold on eternal life. When we were young, we were led about by youthful desires. As children of God, He desires that we grow up into His likeness. God has placed within each of us the potential for greatness, yet many of us live a life of stunted spiritual maturity. We must run as fast as we can away from anything that is contrary to the character of God and to our spiritual well-being.

> *"Flee also youthful lusts: but follow righteousness, faith, charity, peace, with them that call on the Lord out of a pure heart."*
>
> (2 Timothy 2:22 [KJV]).

We must have a pure heart and a clear conscience towards God. We can't follow the lust of the flesh any longer. We must seek peace, love, faith, and Godly character, so these same qualities will follow behind us. The world should acknowledge we're led by God, and our loves should manifest the very nature of heaven on earth. If we're allowing anything else to lead us, we're going in the wrong direction. We must follow after the righteousness of God at all times and at all costs and flee unrighteousness.

A Baby No More

There's a great difference between who we once were and who we are today. Whether you've only recently repented and accepted the sacrifice of Christ or you've walked with Christ for years after you repented of your sins, began a covenant relationship with Christ through baptism in Him name, and received the infilling of the Holy Ghost. No matter where you fall on this continuum, you aren't who you once were.

When we were sinners, we were carnal. We allowed the desires of the flesh to guide our actions. When we first began our relationship with Christ, our flesh was not completely subject to our spirit, even though our spiritual self was alive, and we had a new nature. We were still living in this body of death with all of its old habits and desires.

As young babies in Christ, we were unskilled in righteousness. We didn't understand our new nature. We didn't know the Word of God as intimately as we do now. We've had to grow in grace, truth, and the knowledge of our Lord and Savior, Jesus the Christ. There were some teachings that we weren't able to understand or receive. The milk of the Word nourished us; the simplicity of the Word sustained us in our early walk with Christ.

As we matured, we became more receptive to the depth of righteousness. We were able to take the full weight of the Word and draw strength from it. Paul writes about it in Hebrews in this manner:

> *"For every one that useth milk is unskilful in the word of righteousness: for he is a babe. But strong meat belongeth to them that are of full age, even those who by reason of use have their senses exercised to discern both good and evil."*
>
> (Hebrews 5:13-14 [KJV])

The eloquence of the King James Version of the Bible still resounds with many people today. Many of the younger generations may struggle with the Old English, but the truth in the content of the scriptures still resounds independent of the translation. An unskilled baby can't handle meat.

The International Standard Version puts it in these terms:

"For everyone who lives on milk is still a baby and does not yet know the difference between right and wrong. But solid food is for mature people, whose minds are trained by practice to distinguish good from evil."

(Hebrews 5:13-14)

No matter what version you use, you have to mature in righteousness. We can't continue to live our Christian life as a baby. This isn't God's will. We shouldn't have to spend countless hours determining what course of action we should take in our lives. We shouldn't get into jams, then go to the Word of God to seek a way out of the mess we got ourselves into. The scriptures are not magical spells; we can quote and expect situations in our lives to change. The scriptures are truth that must be lived to become reality.

When we were first born into the Kingdom of God, we didn't know the Word. We weren't expected to understand and live according to all the teachings of righteousness through Christ. However, as we grow up in God, more is required of us. We must begin to trust that all things work together for our good. We must learn to trust that God has a plan for our lives. We must learn to demonstrate the love of Christ to those who use us.

None of this is easy. We must be committed to growing up. We must be willing to learn who God is by studying His Word. There is no cheat code or CliffsNotes that can help. We must apply ourselves to the task. We can't be babies any longer; we must grow up. We must train our minds to distinguish good from evil. We must exercise our righteous character, so it can mature to its full potential.

Our old nature's view of reality was through the lens of sin. This lens was distorted by Adam and Eve's acquisition of the knowledge of good and evil. For us to mature into righteousness, we must correct this lens. We have the knowledge of good and evil within us; we just need to view it through the eyes of righteousness—not sin. The only way this can occur is if we grow up, exercise our new nature, and train our minds to distinguish good from evil.

Correction Brings Righteousness

Everyone remembers being corrected for doing something wrong as a child. It's the Biblical way of raising children. Punishment is a tool to discourage inappropriate behavior. The act of being chastised leads a child to examine his actions. This examination concludes with a desire to avoid future punishment by behaving righteously. Chastisement is an exercise in self-control.

> *"Now no chastening for the present seemeth to be joyous, but grievous: nevertheless, afterward it yieldeth the peaceable fruit of righteousness unto them which are exercised thereby."*
>
> (Hebrews 12:11 [KJV]).

We know when we do something contrary to our new nature, there's an inward stirring from the Holy Ghost. The Holy Ghost causes an internal tugging of our conscience. This conviction leads us to examine our actions and make needed corrections. Punishment is an instructor of righteousness, teaching us to choose the characteristics of our new nature over the desires of our old nature.

The contentment and peace that comes through living a righteous life can't truly be measured. Many people and religious groups have tried to find or develop a path that leads to peace, but the only way to find true peace is through righteousness. We must become the righteousness that was placed within us through the regeneration of the Spirit of God. We must endure the chastisement of God when we don't do what is in agreement with our new nature. We must change our actions when we behave in a way that's contrary to the laws of the Kingdom of God.

God loves us so much. He loves us as we are. He loves us so much that He won't leave us as we are. He desires to lift us up to fulfill the purpose He has for our lives.

> *"For consider him that endured such contradiction of sinners against himself, lest ye be wearied and faint in your minds. Ye have not yet resisted unto blood, striving against sin. And ye have forgotten the exhortation which speaketh unto you as unto children, My son, despise not thou the chastening of the Lord, nor faint when thou art rebuked of him: For whom the Lord loveth he chasteneth, and scourgeth every son whom he receiveth. If ye endure chastening, God dealeth with you as with sons; for what son is he whom the father chasteneth not? But if ye be without chastisement, whereof all are partakers, then are ye bastards, and not sons. Furthermore we have*

had fathers of our flesh which corrected us, and we gave them reverence: shall we not much rather be in subjection unto the Father of spirits, and live? For they verily for a few days chastened us after their own pleasure; but he for our profit, that we might be partakers of his holiness."

(Hebrews 12:3-10 [KJV])

We're going to make mistakes. We're going to experience correction. This is a great thing. If the Lord didn't love us and if we weren't His children, we wouldn't have to worry about receiving discipline. But He loves us. Oh, how He loves us all! We're His children, and He is our good Father. His discipline leads us to become holy even as He is holy. As a disciple of Christ, we must understand that His discipline leads to righteousness.

Live for Righteousness

Righteousness is not an abstract concept. It's not an unattainable level of Godly living that can only be reached by the greatest of people. Righteousness is not a point in time. We don't place ourselves in a church for thirty years, sit on a wooden pew every service, sweat in the summer heat, and freeze in the winter cold, so one day God will pull us out of the oven called the church, and say, "Look here, angels. This one is done! The thermometer says 'Righteous.'"

Righteousness is a way of life. It's how we live out each day and every moment within the day. Righteousness is not a religious practice. It's not learning how to act like a specific denomination. It's not a list of dos and don'ts. It's not who you know. It's not a performance. Righteousness is the living of your regenerated nature.

Christ came to free us from our past, restore to us the liberty that comes only through forgiveness, and empower us to live a life separated unto His purpose.

> *"Who his own self bare our sins in His own body on the tree, that we, being dead to sins, should live unto righteousness: by whose stripes ye were healed"*
>
> (1 Peter 2:24 [KJV])

We did nothing to deserve the gift of salvation. We weren't worthy of the freedom we received through the mercy of God. His mercy took on the punishment we warranted. Mercy gave us liberty, and grace gave us favor with God.

Because He died, we must now live. Our purpose isn't heaven; our reward isn't heaven. Our reward is a crown of eternal life, and our mission is to exhibit the righteousness of God to the world around us. We can't be righteousness locked in a building hidden from sight. We can't live righteousness alone.

Righteousness must be lived out loud. We must live life in complete surrender to the will of God. The fundamentals of a man's character must be developed within the quiet places of a man's heart. However, the true qualities of a man's character are displayed through his actions toward others. The manifestation of one's character through his personal interactions is the litmus test for his level of righteousness.

United in Righteousness

The human body is an amazing, intricate creation. Each part serves a purpose, and each system works to maintain the whole organism. The smallest unit of the body is the cell. These cells join together to form tissues. These tissues combine to form organs. These organs join together to form systems, and these systems work together to maintain life.

Each of us has a function that contributes to the working of Christ's body. We're individual cells united together as a system. We're amalgamated as a driving force to move the Body of Christ toward the manifestation of the Kingdom of God. We are fitly joined together for a purpose.

We must support one another. We can't be righteous alone. We need to be united to fully manifest godly righteousness.

> *"But speaking the truth in love, may grow up into him in all things, which is the head, even Christ: From whom the whole body fitly joined together and compacted by that which every joint supplieth, according to the effectual working in the measure of every part, maketh increase of the body unto the edifying of itself in love."*
>
> (Ephesians 4:15-16 [KJV])

In the garden, God knew it wasn't good for man to be alone, so he created a partner. The same is true in the family of God. It's not good, nor is it possible, for us to be a part of the church alone. We're to be a helpmeet to each other. When we all join together with God, there's nothing that can destroy us. God placed within man the potential for greatness, but this greatness can only be achieved through unity. Unity with God and with each other opens the door to the manifestation of the supernatural.

Just as each cell in the body helps to support the others, just as a man and a woman working together form the powerful foundation of a family, we, too, as members of the church, build one another up.

> *"Wherefore comfort yourselves together, and edify one another, even as also ye do."*
>
> (1 Thessalonians 5:11 [KJV])

We must live in unity to express God's character. Without each other, we can't be righteous. It takes personal interactions and the godly expression of love to mature into our full potential.

Disunity destroys our new nature. The human body functions because each cell knows its place. When one cell becomes out of line, the body begins eliminating the non-compliant cell. In some instances, the cell responds to signals and undergoes a process of death called apoptosis in order to restore the health of the tissue. In other instances, the cell is unresponsive to external signals from the body and becomes a malignant cancer.

Cancer isn't an invading disease; it's your own cells in your own body becoming rebellious and falling out of the unified purpose for which they were designed. We can't afford disunity within the body of Christ. If we can't follow charity with all men and be united in righteousness, we run the risk of jumping from congregation to congregation, spreading our disunity, and becoming a cancer to the body and purpose of Christ. God placed us into the church for a purpose.

I have seen many churches suffer from disunity. The results are devastating to the local congregation. We must bring unity to the church and find a way to establish peace for the church to regain its proper function.

> *"To appoint unto them that mourn in Zion, to give unto them beauty for ashes, the oil of joy for mourning, the garment of praise for the spirit of heaviness; that they might be called trees of righteousness, the planting of the LORD, that he might be glorified."*
>
> (Isaiah 61:3 [KJV])

We gather as a unit. We weren't placed within the church haphazardly. We are the plantings of the Lord.

> *"But now God has set the members, each one of them, in the body just as He pleased."*
>
> (1 Corinthians 12:18 [KJV])

There's a reason we're in the location we find ourselves. It's not to wait out the remainder of our days until the Lord comes after us to warm a seat in the church and barely get by. We need to look around us at where the Lord has placed us in His body and see where we can establish contact with others. We must become tighter with each other and become a driving force for the Kingdom.

We must commit ourselves to building each other up. We must celebrate the accomplishments of those around us. Where there's celebration, there's participation. When we celebrate each other, we'll begin to participate in each other's lives. We need to be an army of encouragers. Sometimes it's not easy; it may cost us. We must lay down our envy and jealousy. We must also sacrifice our time to build each other up.

We must recognize the value of every person. It may be hard to do at times. We've been raised in a society that speaks of equality but pressures us to live a life of prejudice and superiority. Most of our old lifestyle was focused on being better than others, of finding an advantage that would give us the upper hand. Sometimes this came at the cost of flattery.

We'd give a compliment that was not warranted. We must be honest, but we must also understand the cultural climate we're in. From the standpoint of God's perspective, every person is valuable. We must, with love, tell each other of greatness within ourselves and share that God has a plan for our lives. We must ensure we operate out of the righteous motives—love and truth. It's not what we can get out of our interactions with others but what we can do to empower others.

There's great power in the spoken word, and we have the ability, through our words, to speak life and encouragement into others. However, we must ensure our motives are righteous and not self-motivated.

A Righteous Mind

We must keep our focus on what's important. We must prioritize our life. We can't afford to give in to distractions over our God-given purpose. Most of life's dilemmas are the result of a loss of focus on God's divine purpose in our lives. We must know that God is our priority.

One way to determine if this is true is to ask ourselves, "Does our checkbook or schedule reflect that God is my priority?" Are we tithing? Where do we spend most of our money? Do we help others with our resources? If not, we must take the initiative to change this. If we're to grow in righteousness, we must get our priorities straight. Where we spend most of our time and money is a direct reflection of where our heart is.

> *"Therefore if there is any consolation in Christ, if any comfort of love, if any fellowship of the Spirit, if any affection and mercy, fulfill my joy by being like-minded, having the same love, being of one accord, of one mind. Let nothing be done through selfish ambition or conceit, but in lowliness of mind let each esteem others better than himself. Let each of you look out not only for his own interests, but also for the interests of others. Let this mind be in you which was also in Christ Jesus,"*
>
> (Philippians 2:1-5, [KJV])

We must take on the mind of Christ. We must consider others above ourselves. We must humble ourselves and become servants to those God has placed in our lives. We must empty ourselves of pride and self-serving motives. We must examine ourselves to bring every thought into captivity.

> *"Casting down imaginations and every high thing that exalteth itself against the knowledge of God, and bringing into captivity every thought to the obedience of Christ."*
>
> (2 Corinthians 10:5 [KJV])

Growing in righteousness is going to take sacrifice. We must crucify the flesh and its desires. We may even have to put some restraints on our lives simply for the benefit of others. We'll have to limit liberty out of our love for others. We may have the liberty to slam the door, but we must choose not to because of the signal it sends to others. Just because we can do something doesn't mean we should. We must refrain from speaking evil. We don't have to speak quickly just to get the upper hand or win the verbal battle. We must remember we can't take our words back.

> *"If it be possible, as much as lieth in you, live peaceably with all men."*
>
> (Romans 12:18 [NLT])

We must live a life that strives for peace with our fellow man. This is critical to a life of righteousness. We know Christ came to give us peace, not as the world gives peace. We're to give peace to those who are around us. This is a part of what makes us different from the rest of the world. We're set aside for His purpose. The righteous character of our lives should express peace.

> *"Follow peace with all men, and holiness, without which no man shall see the Lord:"*
>
> (Hebrews 12:14 [KJV])

We must also live by faith every day of our lives. What is not of faith is sin. If we aren't living by faith, we run the risk of living life according to our own vanity. We can so easily plan and devise a strategy for our life that seems right to us but is contrary to God's plan and purpose. If we don't live by faith, but we live by sight, we're never going to be able to develop our righteous nature. We must take into captivity our thoughts and evaluate them through a righteous lens. We may need to crucify our own drive for success, recognition, and accolades.

> *"This I say, therefore, and testify in the Lord, that ye henceforth walk not as other Gentiles walk, in the vanity of their mind, having the understanding darkened, being alienated from the life of God through the ignorance that is in them, because of the blindness of their heart."*
>
> (Ephesians 4:17-18 [KJV])

Even Apostle Paul said he had to die daily. He was referring to his thoughts, his own passions, dreams, and desires. We're going to have thoughts and experience events that will elicit a response within us that may be a residue of our old nature. Nevertheless, we must bring these thoughts into subjection to our righteous, new nature.

Thoughts may come, but you determine whether or not the thought stays. You're the landlord of your mind. Serve an eviction notice on the thoughts that don't match the righteous character within your new nature. They shouldn't be there; cast them down. You can't allow toxic thoughts to cloud your mind. You can only grow if you aren't succumbing to a toxic environment.

Righteous maturity is achieved when our spiritual self-controls our thoughts—not our emotions. When we're led by our emotions, our soul is enslaved by our feelings. When we're led by our spiritual nature, our emotions are subject to our spirit. Thoughts give rise to emotions, and when we let our thoughts run wild, our emotions can act irrationally. However, when our emotions are under God's lead, our thoughts prove our spirit is in charge, and people can see it. When our mind, physical body, and emotions are brought under subjection to God, we have the ability to achieve righteous maturity. Whenever part of us is not subject to the new nature, our soul dies to our lustful nature. The righteousness of our new nature can only grow if we keep our mind and body in subjection to the Spirit of God and in love and unity with each other.

Chapter Nine

The Full Stature – The Process of Maturity

"That we henceforth be no more children, tossed to and fro, and carried about with every wind of doctrine, by the sleight of men, and cunning craftiness, whereby they lie in wait to deceive; 15But speaking the truth in love, may grow up into him in all things, which is the head, even Christ:"

(Ephesians 4:14-15 [KJV])

Inevitably, as we go through life, we mature. It's a natural process. From conception to the grave, we're growing and maturing in some way physically and emotionally. It's not a forced event. We don't make ourselves an adult; we grow into an adult. There's a number of factors that can impose limitations on our development, but in the end, we'll reach a level of maturity.

Some people mature at a different rate than others. There are some late bloomers, and there are some that develop emotional and cognitive reasoning that far surpasses their physical age.

Maturation is a multifaceted and complex process. It's a myriad of systems and events working together, set at distinct intervals, which bring about the end product. Growth hormones release at a given time and stimulate a rapid growth phase. These chemical signals elicit additional responses from bone, muscle, and reproductive systems, which work in harmony to propel an adolescent into adulthood.

Our spirit goes through a similar maturing process. Have you ever noticed there are some people who just emanate a natural spiritual maturity? These people may not have been serving God for a long time, or they may have walked with God for decades. Nevertheless, there's just something about them you can feel; they're genuine, unpretentious children of God. They're the real thing.

There are others who may act the part, but there's something that just doesn't ring true about them. There is some level of immaturity in their walk with God. They may have professed to be a follower of Christ all their life, but something is missing. They have learned to emulate others but lack the character required to embody the true maturity of a child of God.

There are those who wear Christianity with a defensive stance, ready at the drop of a hat to argue and fight over their personal beliefs. Wrath and strife are not measures of maturity.

Others will say slanderous things trying to murder the character of other children of God to prove their position in the Kingdom. Some even set themselves upon a seat of judgment to condemn those they feel are not measuring up to the mark they have set. However, slander and judgment aren't measures of maturity. Operating in the works of the flesh to justify your spiritual maturity only serves to prove your lack of maturity.

> *"Now the works of the flesh are manifest, which are these; Adultery, fornication, uncleanness, lasciviousness, idolatry, witchcraft, hatred, variance, emulations, wrath, strife, seditions, heresies, envyings, murders, drunkenness, revellings, and such like: of the which I tell you before, as I have also told you in time past, that they which do such things shall not inherit the kingdom of God."*
>
> (Galatians 5:19-21 [KJV])

You can't reach spiritual maturity utilizing the works of the flesh. Spiritual maturity only comes through spiritual growth. For centuries, modern religion has attempted to develop a formula or a standard operating protocol to manufacture spiritual maturity, but there's no man-made blueprint that can produce spiritual maturity.

The spiritual maturation process is designed to make us like Christ. God's law has been written in the hearts of His children. Through the regeneration of our spirit, we've gained the spiritual genetic potential to grow into the image of Christ. It's already within us. It's not something we have to force to happen; it's something we're born to become.

> *"For this is the covenant that I will make with the house of Israel after those days, saith the Lord; I will put my laws into their mind, and write them in their hearts: and I will be to them a God, and they shall be to me a people."*
>
> (Hebrews 8:10 [KJV])

This transformation was so apparent that the Gentiles began to naturally follow God's law because of the spiritual conversion of their hearts.

> *"For when the Gentiles, which have not the law, do by nature the things contained in the law, these, having not the law, are a law unto themselves: Which shew the work of the law written in their hearts, their conscience also bearing witness, and their thoughts the mean while accusing or else excusing one another;)."*
>
> (Romans 2:14-15 [KJV])

True spiritual maturity can't be achieved in the flesh. We can't emulate it; we must embody it. We can't manufacture it; we must manifest it. We can't achieve it; we must apprehend it within our souls. We must live it, not profess it. We must allow it to flow through us, not pin it to our lapel as an accolade. It's the outward expression of the internal regeneration of our new nature.

The maturation process requires us to actively allow the manifestation of righteousness in our lives. We must choose to be righteous. We must practice the ways of righteousness. The natural processes of spiritual maturity require us to exercise our new spiritual traits—not suppress them. The righteous characteristics of our Father must become preeminent in our lives.

> *"Little children, let no man deceive you: he that doeth righteousness is righteous, even as he is righteous."*
>
> (1 John 3:7 [KJV])

We can't continue to allow our old nature to flourish. We must take every measure to ensure we don't breathe life back into our old selves. We must crucify the remnants of our old nature after our conversion. Paul even spoke of this need in Galatians.

> *"And they that are Christ's have crucified the flesh with the affections and lusts. If we live in the Spirit, let us also walk in the Spirit. Let us not be desirous of vain glory, provoking one another, envying one another."*
>
> (Galatians 5:24-26 [KJV])

Crucifying our fleshly nature is a part of a committed relationship with Christ. Being conceited or jealous of our brothers and sisters in the Lord has no place in the mature life of a child of God. We must put to death such traits. It may take daily work to kill these fleshly characteristics. This is why we've been given the Spirit of God to lead us and to empower us to overcome the old nature and its lust.

Because the maturation process is not a set point but a progressive process that continues throughout our walk with God, we must remember that killing the old nature is not the pinnacle of maturity; it's simply one of the first steppingstones.

> *"Wherefore laying aside all malice, and all guile, and hypocrisies, and envies, and all evil speakings, As newborn babes, desire the sincere milk of the word, that ye may grow thereby: If so be ye have tasted that the Lord is gracious."*
>
> (1 Peter 2:1-3 [KJV])

God has called us His children. We must hold onto this truth. If we begin to lose sight of our identity in Christ, we'll fail to properly mature. We must take an active role in ensuring we're in the right environment and our spiritual nature is protected from influences that can inhibit its growth. We must keep ourselves pure and hold onto the hope that we shall be like Him.

> *"Behold, what manner of love the Father hath bestowed upon us, that we should be called the sons of God: therefore the world knoweth us not, because it knew him not. Beloved, now are we the sons of God, and it doth not yet appear what we shall be: but we know that, when he shall appear, we shall be like him; for we shall see him as he is. And every man that hath this hope in him purifieth himself, even as he is pure."*
>
> (1 John 3:1-3 [KJV])

Not only shall we be like Him when He appears but, in this world, we are like Him. The world may not perceive our nature. They may be blinded by the light of the glorious Gospel that resides within us, but as He is, so are we in this world. We must hold onto this belief, for it defines our identity. Our spiritual characteristics are Christ's nature because that same spirit dwells in us.

> *"Herein is our love made perfect, that we may have boldness in the day of judgment: because as he is, so are we in this world."*
>
> (1 John 4:17 [KJV])

This promise concerning the attributes of our new nature is one of the most powerful realities of who we are. We can't afford to settle for anything less. As we allow the spiritual process of maturity to complete its perfect work, we'll become fully developed into the character of Christ. It may take enduring some things in our lives. There may be some growing pains. If we stay the course and follow the Spirit's lead, we'll have all we need.

> *"But let patience have her perfect work, that ye may be perfect and entire, wanting nothing."*
>
> (James 1:4 [KJV])

We must hold on to these promises. We must take on the task of nurturing our new nature. We must examine ourselves and clean out those things which are not a part of our new nature. We must assign ourselves the purpose to which God has called us.

> *"Having therefore these promises, dearly beloved, let us cleanse ourselves from all filthiness of the flesh and spirit, perfecting holiness in the fear of God."*
>
> (2 Corinthians 7:1 [KJV])

Throughout our walk with God, we'll experience growth and development. We're expected to mature in our walk. We've been given a light to guide us on the path. The light of God's word is an omnipresent force leading us to spiritual maturity. We must walk forward, pressing toward the light. As we progress, our deficits become neutralized. This progression is a natural result of the development of the spiritual genetic potential we received through regeneration. If we fail to be led by the Spirit through the light of this glorious Gospel, we'll wander around in the darkness of this world and become easy prey for the enemy.

> *"This then is the message which we have heard of him, and declare unto you, that God is light, and in him is no darkness at all. If we say that we have fellowship with him, and walk in darkness, we lie, and do not the truth: But if we walk in the light, as he is in the light, we have fellowship one with another, and the blood of Jesus Christ his Son cleanseth us from all sin."*
>
> (1 John 1:5-7 [KJV])

We can't allow outside forces to distract us from our course. We can't tie our efforts into external resources that disconnect us from our source. We can't build upon a foundation other than the cornerstone of Christ. If we are to grow and reach our full potential, we must do so by focusing our attention on the things of God, drawing our strength from the Spirit, and building upon the foundation of Christ.

> *"Ye therefore, beloved, seeing ye know these things before, beware lest ye also, being led away with the error of the wicked, fall from your own stedfastness. But grow in grace, and in the knowledge of our Lord and Saviour Jesus Christ. To him be glory both now and for ever. Amen."*
>
> (2 Peter 3:17-18 [KJV])

As we learn of Christ and the grace He offers, we'll naturally begin to mature. As our relationship with God grows in intimacy, He will reveal more and more about His nature to us. By knowing the nature and traits of our Father, we begin to develop a clearer understanding of what we can and are to become as mature children of God.

Maturity takes time, and it's a process. We must understand that expressing our spiritual characteristics doesn't mean we've maximized our growth potential. When traits begin to develop, they must be exercised to ensure they're strengthened. Genetic potential can provide the code for the building blocks of greatness, but that potential must be actively developed.

The Qualities of Maturing

The level of someone's maturity is not defined by the individual but by comparing his traits to others. Comparisons between members of the church shouldn't be used to boast. Nevertheless, comparisons do allow for introspective assessment of our own spiritual progress. The ultimate comparison is to that of Christ. We must ensure we don't become imitators of each other. We must examine ourselves through the example of Christ.

> *"Examine yourselves, whether ye be in the faith; prove your own selves. Know ye not your own selves, how that Jesus Christ is in you, except ye be reprobates?"*
>
> (2 Corinthians 13:5 [KJV])

We must also be careful not to compare ourselves to ourselves. We must not become imitators because imitation leads to limitation. Imitation is emulation. This is a work of the flesh and is not a sign of maturity. We need examples in our lives to help educate us; we don't need examples for us to replicate. If we imitate, we can never reach greater heights than the model we're using. However, if we learn from the examples before us, we establish a foundation from which we can launch.

> *"For we dare not class ourselves or compare ourselves with those who commend themselves: but they, measuring themselves by themselves, and comparing themselves among themselves, are not wise."*
>
> (2 Corinthians 10:12 [KJV]).

If we're still in need of milk, we're still in an infant state of maturity. We must take an active role in assessing our own spiritual development. If we're not maturing at a proper pace, then we need to examine the factors that may be inhibiting our development.

> *"For when for the time ye ought to be teachers, ye have need that one teach you again which be the first principles of the oracles of God; and*

> *are become such as have need of milk, and not of strong meat. For every one that useth milk is unskilful in the word of righteousness: for he is a babe. But strong meat belongeth to them that are of full age, even those who by reason of use have their senses exercised to discern both good and evil."*
>
> (Hebrews 5:12-14 [KJV])

As we mature, we must take note that there are people behind us who may need our help. We are their examples. Additionally, there are people to whom we look to exemplify the Master. We're all at various stages of spiritual maturity. Nevertheless, there are a few qualities that set the foundation for the maturation process and serve as benchmarks upon which we can stand as we progress toward maturity.

These qualities include not being led by feelings, distinguishing other voices from the voice of God, and not being dependent on the consensus and agreement of others.

Not Being Led by Feelings

Our feelings are *not* the greatest source of truth. Each person perceives events differently, and he responds emotionally based on his personal perception of the events. Not all of these responses are in alignment with the characteristics of God. To be led by our emotions is similar to allowing our fleshly desires to control our actions.

Before our regeneration, our flesh ran the show. The flesh programmed our emotional response to events. When our flesh was attacked or felt mistreated, we felt anger. The emotional programming of our old nature needs to be reprogramed. If we allow our lives to be directed by our emotions, we relinquish control of our spiritual lives to emotional whims.

The Spirit of God must lead us. The Spirit of God is given to us to lead us and guide us into all truth. If the Spirit leads us, we'll not fulfill the lust of the flesh. The leading of the Spirit may feel at first contrary to our natural logic. This is primarily due to the fact that it goes against our emotional perception of reality. Nevertheless, to those who allow the Spirit to lead them as they mature in grace, the leading of the Spirit becomes as natural as being led by your feelings.

There is a period of growing pains associated with this step of maturation because, during this time of development, it's difficult to deny our feelings and trust the Spirit's lead. But we must crucify those feelings and the associated actions that accompany them to ensure the proper spiritual characteristics manifest.

The quality of not being led by our feelings lays a wonderful foundation upon which our faith can rest. Those who've reached this level of maturity can testify to the strength they gained when they allowed the Spirit to lead them rather than their feelings.

Distinguishing Other Voices

There are many voices that speak into our lives. Some of these voices are hard to ignore. Some even speak to us years after the words were verbalized, such as the voice of a mother or father, a trusted mentor, or a friend. Some of these may have served to bring about positive influence; others may still pose obstacles we struggle to overcome. No matter where the voice originated, we have to have an ear to distinguish its source.

Numerous times in the King James translation of the Bible, the phrase, "He that hath an ear let him hear," is written. We must have an ear that hears what the voice of God is saying.

"My sheep hear my voice, and I know them, and they follow me."
(John 10:27 [KJV]).

I know husbands who can sit next to their wife while she holds an entire conversation and never hear a word she said. Some people call it selective hearing. There are some men, however, who can hear their wives simply whisper their name in a crowded room. What makes the difference? Listening.

We often fail to hear the voice of God because we fail to listen to Him speak. He could be shouting at the top of His spiritual lungs, yet we sit in total oblivion to His words. Yet there are times when He speaks to us in a still, quiet voice, and the words resonate like a grand symphony in our soul.

The quality of distinguishing the voice of God from the myriad of other voices in the world only comes through developing an intimate relationship with the Master. There is no other way to learn His voice than to hear it. There is no other way to filter out the nuances of His intonations and intent than to experience them.

With all the voices that resonate in our lives, the ability to focus on the voice of God is a quality of maturity that provides the greatest potential for development. The voice of God must become as prominent as the sound of a foghorn in the mist.

As we begin to mature, developing this quality will require a level of trial and error. At first, we may not know what God's voice sounds like. There may be times when we follow a voice that isn't God's. There may also be times when God's voice is contrary to our own internal voice. In these cases, we have a cloud of witnesses that we can look to for guidance and support.

The Bible is full of people responding and hearing the voice of God. If we train ourselves in the Word of God, we're less likely to be led astray by contrary voices. Additionally, there are people God has placed in our lives that we can rely on to help us distinguish the voice of God.

Spiritual maturity is a team effort. We're not in this thing alone. The devil will try to get us to believe we're alone in this fight and that the only way to grow is in seclusion. However, there's safety in a multitude of counsel. In the end, we must take control of our actions. We can't allow counselors to become another voice adding to the confusion. As we develop our spiritual hearing, those who've gone before us can give us guidance to filter out the distracting voices. In the end, we must learn to hear the voice of God for ourselves.

In truth, the only one who can hear the voice of God in your life is you. As anyone with a testimony of hearing the voice of God will tell you, once you learn to hear His voice, there's nothing that sounds remotely like it. This quality of spiritual maturity is unlike any other and must be experienced to truly be understood. Words written on a page can't convey the effect of knowing that you understand the voice of God. When He speaks to you, the power it has on your spiritual growth is miraculous.

Not Being Dependent on Others' Approval

Most of the time, we want and desire people to support our efforts and to agree with our decisions. However, this doesn't always happen. People won't always agree with our choices. When you throw the aspect of following God into the mix, it increases the probability of disagreement to a new level.

People are naturally led by the flesh. They perceive everyone else through the eyes, ears, emotions, and desires of their fleshly nature. Because of this tendency, when we're following the Spirit's lead, listening to the voice of God is contrary to the fleshly nature of most people. If we're looking for people to support us or provide positive feedback, we're looking in the wrong location. Most of these people have no idea what a spiritual walk looks like or what a proper spiritual decision would be in their own life, let alone someone else's.

We must not fall into the trap of depending on the approval of others to define our spiritual walk. When we begin to lean on the consensus of others, we're no longer leaning on the arm of God. We must hold to the unchanging hand of God. Others may not see the unseen hand of God that is leading us through the path that is before us. They may not foresee the destiny that God has for us. Nevertheless, our anchor is not in the opinion of others but in the approval of God.

As we develop this quality of maturity, we must know we'll face ridicule and scorn. People may say all manner of things against us. The paths that God directs us to follow may not appear to be the most logical or the most advantageous. The Spirit of God may warn us against following other paths that seem logical. We must, with assurance, know His ways are higher than our ways. He knows what He's doing, and His thoughts toward us are with our best interest in mind.

Others may abandon us, and others may defame or slander our name. We must understand they do so out of carnality, not malicious intent. From the surface, it may appear to be different. We must be willing to say, "Father, forgive them for they know not what they do."

Their opinions are not the gale that fills the sails of our spiritual ship. The master of our ship is Christ. He steers our ship, and the gale of the Holy Ghost propels our spiritual life through every tempest that we must endure.

Those who've grown to look beyond the approval of others can testify to all that the only way to truly know yourself is to learn to endure the critics. Following the Spirit's lead will bring out the critics, but it'll also bring your true spiritual character to the surface. This process requires us to see who we truly are within ourselves. It requires us to address the attributes of our lives that are contrary to the new nature we've received. We must deal with the internal conflicts within our soul before we can truly manifest the eternal characteristics of God placed within us through regeneration.

The Benefits of Maturing

There are great benefits to maturing in the Kingdom of God. It gives us access to wonderful gifts, including direct access to the presence of God and to all of God's majesty and power. We must understand we're not carbon copies of each other. We've been regenerated, and the spiritual genetics of our Father has been transferred to our souls, but there remains a remnant of Adam's original nature within us—not his fallen nature but his original design. This is the quality that made us valuable to God—so valuable that He was willing to bankrupt heaven to buy us back.

We're inherently priceless in the eyes of God. He packaged all His glory, all His mercy, all His grace, all His love, all His authority, and power; He stripped Himself of all majesty, became of no reputation, and offered Himself on the cross for us. How priceless are we in the eyes of God?

The greatest benefit to maturing in Christ is becoming the full manifestation of the priceless gem God sees us to be. When the Spirit of God began to move on our hearts, we were a diamond in the rough. However, the hands of the master jeweler, through the cutting and process of maturation, have brought forth the clearest and most perfect diamond of His Kingdom.

We mature into the apple of His eye, the crown jewels of His dynasty, the purest gold that reflects the image of our Master, expressing each of our own unique traits to fulfill our unique calling. We work together in harmony on earth to bring to pass the manifestation of His Kingdom.

> *"But unto every one of us is given grace according to the measure of the gift of Christ. Wherefore he saith, When he ascended up on high, he led captivity captive, and gave gifts unto men. (Now that he ascended, what is it but that he also descended first into the lower parts of the earth? He that descended is the same also that ascended up far above all heavens, that he might fill all things.) And he gave some, apostles; and some, prophets; and some, evangelists; and some, pastors and teachers; For the perfecting of the saints, for the work of the ministry, for the edifying of the body of Christ: Till we all come in the unity of the faith, and of the knowledge of the Son of God, unto a perfect man, unto the measure of the stature of the fulness of Christ: That we henceforth be no more children, tossed to and fro, and carried about with every wind of doctrine, by the sleight of men, and cunning craftiness, whereby they lie in wait to deceive; But speaking the truth in love, may grow up into him in all things, which is the head, even Christ: From whom the whole body fitly joined together and compacted by that which every joint supplieth, according to the effectual working in the measure of every part, maketh increase of the body unto the edifying of itself in love.."*
>
> (Ephesians 4:7-16 [KJV])

The benefits of spiritual maturity allow us to have unwavering faith and trust in God. We can't afford to be children any longer. We can't be an easy mark for the enemy. We must become fully alive in Him. The life of abundance is no longer something about which we sing or talk. It flows from within us—abundant grace, abundant mercy, and abundant favor with God.

These benefits are not just for us as individuals; they're also for the unified body of Christ. The full stature of God's children requires a team. When we're in unity, nothing is impossible to us. When God visited the people, as they were building the tower of Babel, He made an amazing proclamation.

> *"And the LORD said, Behold, the people is one, and they have all one language; and this they begin to do: and now nothing will be restrained from them, which they have imagined to do."*
>
> (Genesis 11:6 [KJV])

There are many benefits to maturity as a child of God, but they all rest upon unity in love. We can't mature alone. We can't manifest the Kingdom of God alone. We can't fulfill our God-given purpose alone. We need each other. Each of us needs to be led by the Spirit of God, hearing the voice of God and seeking His approval in all we do. Since each of us is led by the Spirit, we can accomplish the impossible.

A mature child of God is a decisive benefit to the world. A mature child of God can operate in the authority given to Adam at the beginning. We can cultivate and protect the things of the garden and subdue the things that aren't in godly order. Mature children of God will manifest the Kingdom.

If we unite together in love, the language of the Kingdom, and the purpose of the Kingdom, nothing is impossible for those who believe.

The Eminence of a Mature Son of God

The characteristics of the full stature of our new nature are numerous. The fruits of the Spirit are the foundation upon which all other attributes are expressed. We must bear these fruits as naturally as we breathe.

> *"But the fruit of the Spirit is love, joy, peace, longsuffering, gentleness, goodness, faith, Meekness, temperance: against such there is no law."*
> (Galatians 5:22-23 [KJV])

Allowing our spiritual nature to grow to its full potential gives us unlimited access to the family advantage of being a child of God. The gifts of the Spirit begin to operate within us to the full extent of their power. The gifts of the Spirit, in operation within the church, give us supernatural insight, wisdom, authority, and power that isn't available to the natural world.

> *"But the manifestation of the Spirit is given to every man to profit withal. For to one is given by the Spirit the word of wisdom; to another the word of knowledge by the same Spirit; To another faith by the same Spirit; to another the gifts of healing by the same Spirit; to another the working of miracles; to another prophecy; to another discerning of spirits; to another divers kinds of tongues; to another the interpretation of tongues: But all these worketh that one and the selfsame Spirit, dividing to every man severally as he will."*
> (1 Corinthians 12:7-11 [KJV])

By the Spirit, we have access to revelations and knowledge that can only come from God. We can receive instruction and be educated by the Creator of the universe. We can watch as He performs miracles and healings that aren't possible to mere mortal men.

Additionally, through His great love, we're given the mind of Christ and are filled with the fullness of God. Through the maturation process, we're transformed into the image of Christ.

> *"And to know the love of Christ, which passeth knowledge, that ye might be filled with all the fullness of God."*
>
> (Ephesians 3:19 [KJV])

As mature children of God, we become an eminent part of the Kingdom. We have the mind of Christ; we have the spirit of Christ. The same power that raised Jesus from the dead lives in us. No wonder the devil fights us every step of the way! Through his crucifixion, Christ broke the container that held all the fullness of God. The contents were poured out upon the church, and in one day, the devil had over 3,000 newborn children of God to combat.

The devil is doing his best to keep sinners from coming to the knowledge of Christ and to keep babies in Christ from reaching their full stature. He knows that if we ever realize the eminence we have in this world, his Kingdom will be destroyed.

Full Circle

We are like Christ in this world. As sons and daughters of God, we manifest the life of Jesus. In the garden, the serpent deceived Adam and Eve into believing they were less than what they really were. They lost sight of their identity. We must hold onto the knowledge of who we are in Christ, lest the enemy of our soul deceive us into believing we're less than what God says we are.

God came walking into the garden on the cool of that fateful evening, searching for Adam.

"Adam, where are you?"

God had placed Adam in the position of ultimate dominion, but when God came looking for Adam, Adam was absent. When God finally found him, he was hiding and ashamed. He had tried to cover up his mistake. Nevertheless, he was unable to.

The dominion of the world, the tending of the contents of the garden, the subjugation of the earth was left undone. The destiny of humankind wasn't fulfilled. The identity of man as a child of God was lost.

God desires to place us back into our rightful place, a life where man lives with all he needs. God's Word promises a life with greater abundance. The abundant life is life as it was meant to be in the garden.

We have come full circle on what Adam and Eve had lost. Through Christ, it's been recovered. He has regenerated us so we can take on our rightful place of dominion of the Earth, the Kingdom of our God.

Christ seeks not to subjugate the people of the world but to nurture them and protect them, to cultivate them and bring them to a place of maturity in the Kingdom of our Lord and King. We can't lose sight of our purpose and identity as Adam and Eve did.

We have the knowledge of good and evil within us, and by the Spirit, we have been given the ability to discern what is good and what is evil. When Adam and Eve partook of the tree, the context in which they received the knowledge distorted their view of what was good and what was evil. However, through the maturation process of the Holy Spirit, we're trained by God to be discerners of what is good and what is evil.

> *"But strong meat belongeth to them that are of full age, even those who by reason of use have their senses exercised to discern both good and evil."*
>
> (Hebrews 5:14 [KJV])

We have a great task now ahead of us. We must take the knowledge we have received and the ability to discern between good and evil and step into the role that was left vacated by Adam through his fall. We have a world that is waiting for the children of God.

> *"For the earnest expectation of the creature waiteth for the manifestation of the sons of God."*
>
> (Romans 8:19 [KJV])

Can you hear the voice of God calling to you in the cool of the evening? His sheep know His voice. God has stepped into the garden of your life. He has placed you in His circle, and He is searching for you. He is calling out your name.

"Where are you?" asks God.

He is searching for you. He is looking for you to be positioned where He has called you to be. He looks with expectancy for you to fulfill the destiny He has planned for you.

What will your answer be? Will you even hear His voice? Will your answer be as Adam's?

"Lord, I heard you in the garden, and I hid myself because my soul is naked."

"I had not matured to take on my position of responsibility."

"I was trying to accomplish the task on my own without Your Spirit to lead me."

"Lord, I tried, but the environment I was in was not good."

"This church you placed me in wouldn't let me grow."

"Give me more time. I needed to take care of some other things, and I wasn't maturing as fast as I should've been."

What will be the answer you give the Lord?

On the other hand, will your answer be, "I am here, Lord, tending to those you have left in my care, the remnant of the garden, Adam and Eve's sons and daughters. I am taking on my Father's business."

God will say, "Well done, my good and faithful child."

Fulfilling God's plan for our lives requires spiritual maturity. We can't accomplish it on our own. We need His Spirit living within us, and we need each other. We need to give ourselves fully to His purpose for our lives.

Full stature requires full surrender.

References

Blackwell, K. (2018). "Church Health and Pastoral Tenure Longevity." Retrieved 8-29-2020, 2020, from https://drkevinblackwell.com/2018/09/27/church-health-and-pastoral-tenure-longevity/#:~:text=While%20the%20average%20pastoral%20tenure,most%20crucial%20stage%20for%20revitalization.

Cassidy, S. B. and C. A. Morris (2002). "Behavioral phenotypes in genetic syndromes: genetic clues to human behavior." Adv Pediatr 49: 59-86.

Chen, M. and L. Zhang (2011). "Epigenetic mechanisms in developmental programming of adult disease." Drug Discov Today 16(23-24): 1007-1018.

Churchill, F. B. (1974). "William Johannsen and the genotype concept." J Hist Biol 7(1): 5-30.

Dhana, K., J. Haines, G. Liu, C. Zhang, X. Wang, A. E. Field, J. E. Chavarro and Q. Sun (2018). "Association between maternal adherence to healthy lifestyle practices and risk of obesity in offspring: results from two prospective cohort studies of mother-child pairs in the United States." BMJ 362: k2486.

Dukes, A. and G. Palm (2019). "Reproductive justice and support for young fathers." Infant Ment Health J 40(5): 710-724.

Guidolin, D., D. Anderlini, M. Marcoli, P. Cortelli, G. Calandra-Buonaura, A. S. Woods and L. F. Agnati (2019). "A New Integrative Theory of Brain-Body-Ecosystem Medicine: From the Hippocratic Holistic View of Medicine to Our Modern Society." Int J Environ Res Public Health 16(17).

Hancock, K. J., D. Lawrence and S. R. Zubrick (2014). "Higher maternal protectiveness is associated with higher odds of child overweight and obesity: a longitudinal Australian study." PLoS One 9(6): e100686.

Holliday, R. (1990). "DNA methylation and epigenetic inheritance." Philos Trans R Soc Lond B Biol Sci 326(1235): 329-338.

Jeffreys, B. (2019). Do children in two-parent families do better? BBC News, BBC News.

Lipton, B. H. (2005). The biology of belief: unleashing the power of consciousness, matter and miracles. Santa Rosa, CA, Mountain of Love/Elite Books.

Lipton, B. H. and S. Bhaerman (2010). Spontaneous Evolution: Our Positive Future and a Way to Get There From Here, Hay House Inc.

McLanahan, S., L. Tach and D. Schneider (2013). "The Causal Effects of Father Absence." Annu Rev Sociol 39: 399-427.

Sallon, S., E. Cherif, N. Chabrillange, E. Solowey, M. Gros-Balthazard, S. Ivorra, J. F. Terral, M. Egli and F. Aberlenc (2020). "Origins and insights into the historic Judean date palm based on genetic analysis of germinated ancient seeds and morphometric studies." Sci Adv 6(6): eaax0384.

Simpson, N. S., E. L. Gibbs and G. O. Matheson (2017). "Optimizing sleep to maximize performance: implications and recommendations for elite athletes." Scand J Med Sci Sports 27(3): 266-274.

Strong, J. (2010). The New Strong's Expanded Exhaustive Concordance of the Bible, Thomas Nelson.

Ungerer, M., J. Knezovich and M. Ramsay (2013). "In utero alcohol exposure, epigenetic changes, and their consequences." Alcohol Res 35(1): 37-46.

Wang, Y., J. Min, J. Khuri and M. Li (2017). "A Systematic Examination of the Association between Parental and Child Obesity across Countries." Adv Nutr 8(3): 436-448.

www.ingramcontent.com/pod-product-compliance
Lightning Source LLC
Chambersburg PA
CBHW072016070526
44583CB00015B/1501